MW01205023

From
Shame
to Fame

Bishop Gray McIntosh

Zeph 3: 19

From Shame To Fame

By
Gary McIntosh

Scripture quotations noted NKJV are from
THE NEW KING JAMES VERSION © 1979, 1980, 1982
Thomas Nelson, Inc., Publishers.

Scripture quotations noted The Message Bible are taken from
THE MESSAGE © 1993, 1994, 1995, 1996, 2000, 2001, 2002.
Used by permission of NavPress Publishing Group.

Scripture quotations noted NLT are taken from the Holy Bible,
New Living Translation, copyright © 1996. Used by permission of
Tyndale House Publishers, Inc.,
Wheaton, Illinois 60189.
All rights reserved.

Scripture quotations noted The Amplified® Bible,
copyright © 1954, 1958, 1962, 1965, 1987 by
The Lockman Foundation. Used by permission. (www. Lockman.org)

Neither the publisher or the author is engaged in rendering professional advice or services to the individual reader. The ideas, procedures, and suggestions in this book are not intended as a substitute for consulting with a licensed professional. All matters regarding your mental health require professional supervision. Neither the author nor the publisher shall be liable or responsible for any loss or damage allegedly arising from any information or suggestion in this book. While the author has made every effort to provide accurate Internet addresses at the time of publication, neither the publisher nor the author assumes any responsibility for errors or for changes that occur after publication.

Contents

Introduction   1

Part One: Why the Story   3

Chapter 1:   If God Says You're A King, You Are!   5
Chapter 2:   Touch Not Mine Anointed   15
Chapter 3:   To Whom Can I Show Kindness?   21

Part Two: Experiencing Shame   27

Chapter 4:   The Name of Shame   29
Chapter 5:   What's the Difference in Shame?   33
Chapter 6:   The Other Type of Shame   39
Chapter 7:   The Marks and Behaviors of Shame   51
Chapter 8:   Recovery From Shame   61
Chapter 9:   Transferring Out of Shame-Based Behaviors   73

Part Three: After the Deliverance   81

Chapter 10:   Loyalty and Betrayal   83
Chapter 11:   David, Mephibosheth, and Ziba   87
Chapter 12:   Deception and Betrayal   91
Chapter 13:   The Defiance of the Betrayer   93
Chapter 14:   The Challenge to be Loyal   101

Living Free   107

Part Four: A Necessary Addition   109

Chapter 15:   A Church in Crisis   111
Chapter 16:   How Did It Begin?   115
Chapter 17:   It All Comes Back to Christ   121

About the Author   125

"GUILT IS WHEN YOU FEEL BAD FOR WHAT YOU'VE DONE. SHAME IS WHEN YOU FEEL BAD FOR WHO YOU ARE."

GARY MCINTOSH

Introduction

Have you found yourself suffering with issues of shame and guilt? You're not alone. A recent survey of pastors who do counseling concluded that other than marital strife, guilt and shame are the most frequent issues they deal with in counseling.

How do you get set free? That's what this book is about. This teaching will show how shame gets in us, how it will manifest in our life and personality, and how God will deliver and heal us from it. This is a crucial word to help you overcome, get the victory, be set free, and never look back to the old life again.

It's important to lay a foundation for you. Most of this teaching will come from 1 and 2 Samuel as it recounts events in the life of David, both before and during the time he was king over Israel. Others enter the story also. It's from these others we will see how one went from shame to fame. I will also reference Zephaniah, who delivered a prophetic word to Israel. That prophetic word has an important implication for us today.

If you are not accustomed to lessons drawn from the Old Testament texts, remember this verse:

"For whatever things were written before were written for our learning, that we through the patience (perseverance) and comfort of the Scriptures might have hope." Romans 15:4 NKJV

Hope is the purpose for writing this book… hope for you today, and hope for your future.

Why the Story?

Sometimes we wonder why there are certain stories in the Bible. We find in a few chapters of one of the books of the Bible where someone is mentioned and then never heard from again in the rest of the Bible.

The verse we most remember that commends all of the Bible to us is:

"All Scripture is given by inspiration of God, and is profitable for doctrine, for reproof, for correction, for instruction in righteousness, that the man of God may be complete, thoroughly equipped for every good work."   2 Timothy 3:16-17 *NKJV*

Let's pick up on the part in verse 17, *"...that the man (or woman) of God may be complete."*

How does Scripture work by the hand of God to make us complete? My view is it provides a pathway for understanding about how in our own circumstances God is at work redeeming us. The Scripture is there so we can understand the reality of God's promises to us.

Scripture also works to provide examples of how other people react when someone is redeemed. These examples work to cultivate wisdom and understanding in us. We become *thoroughly equipped.*

Much of the Bible is filled with stories. These true accounts are of events that actually happened. These real events come down to us as stories for us to study, meditate on, and learn from. They are tools from the hand of God to reveal His glory, His mercy, His grace, and His love for us.

Chapter 1

IF GOD SAYS YOU'RE A KING, YOU ARE!

The promises given to us in Scripture are amazing...so amazing that it's difficult to believe how great and grand God's gifts and promises to us really are. That becomes the challenge and dilemma we face as Christians. Will we really believe God and accept His love, or will we cling in unbelief to our past and our old conditions?

To repent and believe that God has forgiven us is fundamental to our life in Christ. The next thing to believe is that God really does have a plan, a hope, and a future for us. It's our resistance to believing these wonderful promises that prevents our growth and progress as new creatures in Christ.

We can't continue to hang onto our old concepts and beliefs and possess the promises Christ has given us. We will either wear a robe of filthy rags, or we will wear a garment of salvation and a robe of righteousness.

That's what we will begin to see with Saul, the first king over Israel. But first we need to know about David and Jonathan.

In 1 Samuel we have a very interesting story. The nation of Israel was at war. Their enemy at this point of time was the Philistine army. Israel was watching them as they came near.

As soon as the lad had gone, David arose from a place toward the south, fell on his face to the ground, and bowed down three times. . . 1 Samuel 20:41 NKJV

It's in this verse and the next we see the covenant made by Jonathan and David.

Then Jonathan said to David, "Go in peace, since we have both sworn in the name of the Lord, saying, 'May the Lord be between your descendants and my descendants, forever." So he arose and departed, and Jonathan went into the city.
1 Samuel 20:42 NKJV

By the time David had finished reporting to Saul, Jonathan was deeply impressed with David; an immediate bond was forged between them. He became totally committed to David; from that time on he would be David's number one advocate and friend.
1 Samuel 18:1 The Message Bible

From that beginning, their relationship as friends and brothers grew into a pledge of covenant. They had a problem, though. Jonathan's father was Saul, who was the king. Saul realized that God had anointed David as king. Saul wanted his son, Jonathan, to be king. God had other plans.

Saul wasn't looking to be a king, and when the time came to crown him king, they found him hiding. He was making all the excuses he could to say that God's will shouldn't be done.

Saul answered (to Samuel), "But I'm only a Benjaminite, from the smallest of Israel's tribes, and from the most insignificant clan in the tribe at that. Why are you talking to me like this?"
1 Samuel 9:20 The Message Bible

We all make excuses to God. We say we're not perfect and can't be used by Him. It's like we've all told God, *"Why are you talking to me like this?"*

So here is where we are held back by shame. It becomes such a bondage, we never release ourselves to the promise God has for our life. We see ourselves with an imperfect heart, but God sees us through the perfect, Jesus, and His love for us. We'll explore shame more fully in future chapters.

Saul allowed his old sin nature to constantly flare up, and ultimately he chose the flesh over the Spirit. He was king until he disobeyed God.

Samuel gives the account of Saul's disobedience and God's decision to remove him as king and anoint another (David) in his place.

Saul disobeyed God; that disobedience came from a heart that wasn't willing to accept God's approval and blessing. The disobedience came from a heart that placed the approval of men above the approval of God.

God began to look for a man after His own heart. He sent Samuel to Jesse the Bethlehemite. Samuel looked at each of Jesse's sons and said, "No, not Eliab; no, not Adinadab; no, not Shammah. . . " Samuel looked at seven of Jesse's sons. God had chosen this family for a promise, a lineage, and a kingdom.

Samuel finally asked Jesse, "Are all the young men here?" Jesse said, "There's the youngest; he's out tending the sheep." Samuel replied, "We will not sit down until he comes here."

When you're in God's timing, everything stops until you are where God can bless you with the promise of His kingdom. Nobody did anything else until David was brought in from tending the sheep.

When we think of a young man tending sheep, doing the work of a shepherd, it's all too easy to think of a quiet pastoral scene with a flowing stream, lush grass, and quiet sheep. Nothing could be further from the truth.

Sheep are dumb. They will follow anything, and danger is ever present. A shepherd must be on guard every minute. He must protect them; sheep can't defend themselves from the wolves and the bears. A shepherd has to lead them to the grass and the water so they are fed and nourished. Sheep don't have the sense to know where it is on their own.

With all these problems, you can't get angry at the sheep because you have to do these things for them. Sheep are sheep, and sheep are just that way.

That's why David's job as a shepherd was the right training ground. If he could shepherd sheep, then he could shepherd a nation.

So he sent and brought him in. Now he was ruddy, with bright eyes, and good-looking. And the Lord said, "Arise, anoint him; for this is the one!" 1 Samuel 16:12 NKJV

Back to our story. David was running from Saul because Saul was trying to kill him. Saul didn't want David to succeed him as king. He wanted his own son, Jonathan, to become king. Saul wanted the kingdom to stay in his family, not go to another's.

What's going on here? Saul disobeyed God. God removed the anointing because of Saul's disobedience and anointed another in his place. This grieved Saul. In his distress, he sought to kill the one who had received the anointing.

This is a pattern we want to observe and learn from. It's so important that we will cover this later in the book.

Now he was throwing spears at David…trying to run after him, trying to find and locate him and make the plans of God a plan of the flesh.

Satan throws the world in front of us; he pursues our weaknesses and wants to steal our peace. He forces us through our wrong self-image to fight back with a plan of the flesh.

How often do we try to make God's plan a plan of the flesh because we won't believe we are "sitting in heavenly places" with him? We don't believe that we are "joint heirs" with him. Our shame won't let us dream or believe what God has said to us. So we make a plan of flesh instead.

Jonathan and David are in the field talking. Jonathan had previously talked with his father. Saul told him, "No, I won't kill him." But Saul didn't keep his word.

> *David got out of Naioth in Ramah alive and went to Jonathan. "What do I do now? What wrong have I inflicted on your father that makes him so determined to kill me?" "Nothing,"* *said Jonathan. "You've done nothing wrong. And you're not going to die. Really, you're not! My father tells me everything. He does nothing, whether big or little, without confiding in me. So why would he do this behind my back? It can't be." But David said, "Your father knows that we are the best of friends, so he says to himself, 'Jonathan must know nothing of this. If he does, he'll side with David.' But it's true; as sure as God lives, and as sure as you're alive before me right now, he's determined to kill me."*
> 1 Samuel 20:1-3 The Message Bible

As it turns out, Saul *was* trying to kill David, and Jonathan was heart broken. Jonathan finally understood that his father Saul wanted David dead. The Bible says they wept with each other.

> *Then Jonathan said to David, "Go in peace, since we have both sworn in the name of the Lord, saying, 'May the Lord be between you and me. And between your descendants and my descendants, forever.'" So he arose and departed, and Jonathan went into the city.* 1 Samuel 20:42 NKJV

The promise made between David and Jonathan was the last thing spoken between them. From then on, the course of their lives would take dramatically different directions.

As we continue the story, the Philistines were coming, and Saul understood that his days were numbered. He knew his death was at hand.

Saul was still the king. He'd lost God's anointing, but he was still in the position of king. He was moving in his own strength because God's strength wasn't with him any longer. His own strength wasn't sufficient strength. There must be a source of strength he could get to. Because God's strength had left him, he had to find a substitute. However, nothing can substitute for God's strength.

On his own, he sought out a witch, the witch of Endor. Not only did he seek out a witch (this all occurs in 1st Samuel chapter 27), he attempted to disguise himself so the witch would not know it was him.

When we disobey God, when we seek our plan instead of His, when we try to work out of our strength instead of His, we have our ears closed to the voice of God.

We often find ourselves stressed, pressured, or perhaps out of control. This usually occurs because we stopped believing in God's promise and provision for us. We want what God promises, but on our own terms, not believing that God will truly deliver what He said He would.

What most people do is complain to friends and relatives, and they are only too happy to give their advice. There's only one problem here. We've gone to the wrong source!

Prayer, fasting and seeking God with your whole heart is the last thing on your mind. Like Saul, you know you have a throne, but unwilling to believe God for how your life should go, you lose God's authority and start relying on your powerless position of flesh.

The prophets can't give a word to that which God has not blessed, the flesh plan. The witch of Endor couldn't get a word for Saul because God's hand was not on her. Saul couldn't get a word because God was not speaking to him, not even in his dreams.

God had already spoken to him, and he refused to believe it and receive it completely! Saul was in the consequences of his flesh plan. God had spoken to him, but Saul disobeyed God. Now Saul had lost his position as king over Israel.

In Saul's frustration, he went to the witch, asking for a word. He told her to call up Samuel and to ask him for a word.

Then Samuel said, "So why do you ask me, seeing the Lord has departed from you and has become your enemy?

And the Lord has done for himself as He spoke by me. For the Lord has torn the kingdom out of your hand and given it to your neighbor, David.

Because you did not obey the voice of the Lord nor execute His fierce wrath upon Amalek, therefore the Lord has done this thing to you this day.

Moreover the Lord will also deliver Israel with you into the hand of the Philistines. And tomorrow you and your sons will be with me. The Lord will also deliver the army of Israel into the hand of the Philistines." 1 Samuel 28:16-19 NKJV

Shock set in. Put in other words, "You're going to die, and your sons (including Jonathan) are about to lose their lives in battle also!"

The Philistines made war on Israel. The men of Israel were in full retreat from the Philistines, falling left and right, wounded on Mount Gilboa. The Philistines caught up with Saul and his sons. They killed Jonathan, Abinadab, and Malki-Shua, Saul's sons.

The battle was hot and heavy around Saul. The archers got his range and wounded him badly. Saul said to his weapon bearer, "Draw your sword and put me out of my misery, lest these pagan pigs come and make a game out of killing me."

But his weapon bearer wouldn't do it. He was terrified. So Saul took the sword himself and fell on it. When the weapon bearer saw that Saul was dead, he too fell on his sword and died with him. So Saul, his three sons, and his weapon bearer, the men closest to him, died together that day. 1 Samuel 31:1-6 The Message Bible

There is an old spiritual hymn that says, "Where could I go but to the Lord?" This psalmist realized his place in the Lord. He realized his position, and he realized it wasn't who he was, but who He is that made him see the only counsel he could seek was in the Lord. "Needing a friend who will love me till the end, where could I go but to the Lord?"

Jesus has a covenant with you, and if He says, "Come up here with me," you are worthy! You are not the least of the tribes as Saul said, but you are washed in the blood of Jesus and standing before Him. If you continue to carry your shame and guilt, you will never answer Him, but constantly make excuses why you can't respond to His call.

There is no condemnation to those who are in Christ Jesus. He is waiting to hear your reply, "Yes, Lord, I'll be right there!"

IF CHRIST SAYS YOU'RE A KING, YOU ARE!

Chapter 2

TOUCH NOT MINE ANOINTED

God had his hand on Saul, even in his sinful state. Saul knew this. Saul knew that God had decreed a righteous judgment. God also had his hand on David. Fearful and running scared, David knew that God was in control.

Saul, even as king, never accepted who he was and could be in God. David did know who Saul was as God's appointed king.

Now it happened, when Saul had returned from following the Philistines, that it was told him, saying, "Take note! David is in the Wilderness of En Gedi."

Then Saul took three thousand chosen men from all Israel, and went to seek David and his men on the Rocks of the Wild Goats.

So he came to the sheepfolds by the road, where there was a cave; and Saul went in to attend to his needs. (David and his men were staying in the recesses of the cave.)

Then the men of David said to him, "This is the day of which the Lord said to you, 'Behold, I will deliver your enemy into your hand, that you may do to him as it seems good to you.'" And David arose and secretly cut off a corner of Saul's robe.

Now it happened afterward that David's heart troubled him because he had cut Saul's robe.

And he said to his men, "The Lord forbid that I should do this thing to my master, the Lord's anointed, to stretch out my hand against him, seeing he is the anointed of the Lord."

So David restrained his servants with these words, and did not allow them to rise against Saul. And Saul got up from the cave and went on his way. 1 Samuel 24:1-7 NKJV

David had a reason to run from Saul every time he turned around. He was tricked into fighting the Philistines, was attacked by the king, and was constantly hunted.

Finally, David thought he could rest with his men for a little bit. They found a cave. They went deep inside so they could hide. They were worn out and without sleep. God knows just when to test us. Finally, at rest in the cave, and who showed up? Saul!

David knew better than to touch Saul. Saul was still the king. As far as David was concerned, you don't mess with God's servant.

Temptation can come from the friendliest places. This time it came from David's own men.

Then the men of David said to him, "This is the day of which the Lord said to you, 'Behold, I will deliver your enemy into your hand, that you may do to him as it seems good to you." 1 Samuel 24:4 NKJV

Temptation can look like the smart thing to do. It can look like the right thing to do. The problem is, temptation usually leads to the wrong thing to do.

David ended up cutting off part of Saul's robe. David knew better than that. David was responding to temptation. It wouldn't be the last time in his life that he gave in to temptation.

Look at his response to his disobedience:

Immediately, he felt guilty. He said to his men, "God forbid that I should have done this to my master, God's anointed, that I should so much as raise a finger against. He's God's anointed!" David held his men to check with these words and wouldn't let them pounce on Saul. Saul got up, left the cave and went on down the road. 1 Samuel 24:5-7 The Message Bible

David's men didn't respect God's anointing on Saul, but David did. It's one of the things that confirmed his anointing; he respected the anointing Saul carried. That's a testimony to David's walk with God. He was walking with a fear of God. He knew what his disobedience was and was quick to repent of it.

Later, after Saul and his sons died in battle (1 Samuel 31), a young soldier showed up at David's camp.

Shortly after Saul died, David returned to Ziklag from his rout of the Amalekites. Three days later a man showed up unannounced from Saul's army camp.

Disheveled and obviously in mourning, he fell to his knees in respect before David. David asked, "What brings you here?"

He answered, "I've just escaped from the camp of Israel."

"So what happened?" said David. "What's the news?"

He said, "The Israelites have fled the battlefield, leaving a lot of their dead comrades behind. And Saul and his son Jonathan are dead."

David pressed the young soldier for details: "How do you know for sure that Saul and Jonathan are dead?"

"I just happened by Mount Gilboa and came on Saul, badly wounded and leaning on his spear, with enemy chariots and horsemen bearing down hard on him. He looked behind him, saw me, and called me to him 'Yes sir,' I said, 'at your service.' He asked me who I was, and I told him, 'I'm an Amalekite.'"

"Come here," he said, "and put me out of my misery; I'm nearly dead already, but my life hangs on."

"So I did what he asked—I killed him. I knew he wouldn't last much longer anyway. I removed his royal headband and bracelet, and have brought them to my master. Here they are."

In lament, David ripped his clothes to ribbons. All the men with him did the same. They wept and fasted the rest of the day, grieving the death of Saul and his son Jonathan, and also the army of God and the nation Israel, victims in a failed battle.

Then David spoke to the young soldier who had brought the report: "Who are you, anyway?"

"I'm from an immigrant family—an Amalekite."

"Do you mean to say," said David, "that you weren't afraid to up and kill God's anointed king?" Right then he ordered one of his soldiers, "Strike him dead!" The soldier struck him, and he died.

"You asked for it," David told him. "You sealed your death sentence when you said you killed God's anointed king."
2 Samuel 1:1-16 The Message Bible

This young soldier, who knew nothing of the fear of God, nothing of a knowledge of God, thought he had performed a great service for David. Not knowing God, or a fear of God, he thought he really knew David's mind concerning Saul.

This is a good example of religious pretense. Religious thought, outside of a knowledge of God and a fear of God, always goes after God's anointed.

In the New Testament, this is shown to an even greater extreme when the religious leaders of the day sought to kill Jesus. Christ is the enemy of the religious, and they always seek to crucify Him.

There is an idea going around these days that if anyone says anything contrary to what a major minister or ministry says, "Well, just don't you touch God's anointed!"

If you're not speaking in love, watch out. But if you are speaking in love and walking in the fear of God, then don't worry. You have the same anointing inside yourself that every other born again man or woman of God has. *You are anointed and in Christ.*

But you have an anointing from the Holy One, and you know all things. 1 John 2:20 NKJV

In the era of Saul and David, very few received an anointing from God: the prophets, the king (who received his anointing from God through the prophet), and the priests. No one else received it.

As redeemed people who are covered by the blood of Christ, all of us have received an anointing from Him. It's in us, every one of us.

Be humble; seek the Lord. Walk in the fear of the Lord. You're just as anointed as any other child of God. It's really okay to have the freedom, under God, to possess your own mind about things. After all, you have been transformed by the renewing of your mind in Christ.

Chapter 3

TO WHOM CAN I SHOW KINDNESS?

D avid had become king over both Judah and Israel. David began to remember his old friend Jonathan. He remembered the covenant between them and the love they had for each other as brothers.

> *Now David said, "Is there still anyone who is left of the house of Saul, that I may show him kindness for Jonathan's sake?"*
>
> *And there was a servant of the house of Saul whose name was Ziba. So when they had called him to David, the king said to him, "Are you Ziba?" And he said, "At your service!"*
>
> *Then the king said, "Is there not still someone of the house of Saul, to whom I may show the kindness of God?" and Ziba said to the king, "There is still a son of Jonathan who is lame in his feet."* 2 Samuel 9:1-3 NKJV

Ziba didn't even say his name; he just identified his condition.

> *So the king said to him, "Where is he?" And Ziba said to the king, "Indeed he is in the house of Machir the son of Ammiel, in Lo Debar."* 2 Samuel 9:4 NKJV

As you read through these chapters in 1st and 2nd Samuel and elsewhere in the Bible, you'll twist your tongue around a lot of unusual names. All of these names have meanings. We're going to learn some of their meanings as we go along.

The place that Jonathan's son was at is called "Lo Debar." Lo Debar means "dry place" in Hebrew.

Jonathan's son was in a dry place. Have you ever been in a dry place yourself? When you're there, it seems impossible to get yourself out of it. The dry place is a place of no hope.

What do you do with yourself now? Nothing works. And no one seems able to help. That's the predicament Jonathan's son was in.

David did something about Jonathan's son in the dry place. He brought him up out of there and into his palace.

Then King David sent and brought him out of the house of Machir the son of Ammiel, from Lo Debar.
Now when Mephibosheth the son of Jonathan, the son of Saul, had come to David, he fell on his face and prostrated himself. Then David said, "Mephibosheth?" And he answered, "Here is your servant!" 2 Samuel 9:5-6 NKJV

Mephibosheth (Me-phĭb'o-shĕth) only knew living with feet that were lame, and living in a dry place. However, Mephibosheth did walk in the fear of God. He probably knew about his father's covenant with David. But that was not the basis for approaching the king that God had anointed. Little did he know the favor of the king was about to come to him.

So David said to him, "Do not fear, for I will surely show you kindness for Jonathan your father's sake, and will restore to you all the land of Saul your grandfather; and you shall eat bread at my table continually."

Then he bowed himself, and said, "What is your servant, that you should look upon such a dead dog as I?" 2 Samuel 9:7-8 NKJV

Mephibosheth thought of himself as something lost and forgotton, not worth anyone's attention. But he was worthy of David's attention. He was in a lineage where covenant had been established with David, and David was committed to remembering his covenant with Jonathan.

What about Saul's other sons? There were a number of other sons from Saul's house, but none were held in the same regard as Jonathan. David only made covenant with Jonathan, not with any of Jonathan's brothers.

Because of covenant, Mephibosheth was brought up out of the dry place. Because of covenant, he was brought into the king's palace. Because of covenant, he and his family would have a place at the king's table for the rest of their lives.

After this deliverance out of the dry place, after the restoration of his inheritance, something even more incredible happened.

And the king called to Ziba, Saul's servant, and said to him, "I have given to your master's son all that belonged to Saul and to all his house."

"You, therefore, and your sons and your servants, shall work the land for him, and you shall bring in the harvest, that your master's son may have food to eat. But Mephibosheth, your master's son, shall eat bread at my table always." Now Ziba had fifteen sons and twenty servants.

Then Ziba said to the king, "According to all that my lord the king has commanded his servant, so will your servant do." "As for Mephibosheth," said the king, "he shall eat at my table like one of the king's sons."

Mephibosheth had a young son whose name was Micha. And all who dwelt in the house of Ziba were servants of Mephibosheth.

So Mephibosheth dwelt in Jerusalem, for he ate continually at the king's table. And he was lame in both his feet.
2 Samuel 9:9-13 NKJV

David, in raising Mephibosheth up and out of his dry place, gave him his father's servants. Moreover, he gave him all his father's servant's sons, and all his father's servant's servants. That should be enough: about 35 workers in all.

They were assigned to work the land originally owned by Saul. That land, by royal decree, was now owned by Mephibosheth. He got grandad's land *and* grandad's servants.

What is their assignment? *To bring in the harvest!* Who do they bring in the harvest for? Mephibosheth, whose father Jonathan was in covenant with King David.

Mephibosheth's son, Micha, is mentioned in verse 12. You want to know why? Because the blessings received by the father get shared by the son also.

Years ago, out in California, there used to be an electronics store that sold big screen TVs. The ad campaign featured the owner of the store. He referred to himself as the king of big screen televisions. His tag line was "It's good to be the king!"

So it is. It's also good to be in a covenant with the King. The King's desire is to remember His covenant with you.

Later in the book, we will revisit this part of our story. There are important issues that come up between David, Mephibosheth, and Ziba. We see hearts revealed.

Before that, as we start our next chapter, we get to the heart of our story. We take another look at names. . .

Experiencing Shame

A person living with shame only knows half a life. The bondage he is experiencing takes him into dry places in life where hope and personal freedom seem to be non-existent.

In this next section, we're going to explore what shame is exactly, learning how it begins in us and how it affects our life, discovering that there is more than one way it can manifest in us. Shame has strongholds that it anchors to the inside of us. Those strongholds become tools used by shame to control our life.

We'll learn about another side of shame and how that side of shame is planted in our hearts. As we see what the seeds of shame are, we will understand how to keep our lives free of them.

What becomes vitally important then, is knowing how shame affects our personality and behaviors, how shame drives us.

God gives us hope, though, as we will soon see. Recovery from shame by the hand of God takes many forms. We're going to see a number of them. God is there to show us how we can take specific, positive steps to emerge from bondage into freedom.

God's heart for us is to live free from shame and step out of the past which has held us captive. Let's go to chapter four and let the healing begin.

Chapter 4

THE NAME OF SHAME

Our story, up to now, has taken us through the anointing of Saul as king, the turbulence of his reign, and his downfall. We've also looked at the relationship between David and Jonathan, the covenant forged between them, and how David continued to honor that covenant after Jonathan's death.

The story continued with Mephibosheth, his son, and Ziba, along with Ziba's family and servants. Ziba was originally Saul's servant, but he had been reassigned by David to serve Mephibosheth.

Let's look again at how the names of people and places have meaning. This was (and is) particularly important in Jewish culture. Our interest now is how important people's names are.

Names expressed a person's heritage. A name could tell where a person's family came from. A name could express his condition. His name described him to the world around him. It also told that person about himself or herself.

Every time a person heard his name, it was as though he was hearing a prophecy about himself. People *knew* what his name meant.

Let's take David's name as an example. The name David in Scripture means "beloved." Every time his father or mother would call to him, he would identify that they were calling him "beloved." That became David's identity. It became David's reality.

This is the connection to the central theme of this book. . . . learning what Mephibosheth's name meant.

It so happened that Saul's son, Jonathan, had a son who was maimed in both feet. When he was five years old, the report on Saul and Jonathan came from Jezreel. His nurse picked him up and ran, but in her hurry to get away, she fell, and the boy was maimed. His name was Mephibosheth. 2 Samuel 4:4 The Message Bible

The nurse had just heard about the death of Mephibosheth's father, Jonathan, and his grandfather, Saul. Knowing that the Philistines likely wouldn't stop at father and son, but would attempt to go after the grandson (and her), she took Mephibosheth as a tender five-year-old child and ran. In her anxiety and haste, she fell. That fall maimed Mephibosheth. The physical disfigurement and handicap became his shame.

You see, Mephibosheth's name means, "breathing shame." From his earliest memories, every time his nurse called him, he would hear, "Come here, one who breathes shame." It wasn't even a situation he had control over, but it became his identity. When his name was spoken to him, he knew nothing else but to internalize it.

There's some common words we associate with shame. Look at a few of them:

Disgrace. The prefix "dis" means "without," thus "without grace." It's horrible to live without the grace of God. To live in shame is to live without grace.

Humiliation. Did you ever feel like after you messed something up that you "had egg on your face"? That's humiliation in a mild way. Humiliation can come to us in much more severe ways. A humiliation can alter the course of a person's life; it's such a powerful thing. The response to humiliation is usually to be affected by shame.

Remorse. We can have remorse over the sin in our lives. When prompted by the Holy Spirit, remorse will lead us to repentance. But we can also have remorse over bad choices we've made. Mistakes about decisions made can lead to remorse. Again, our response to remorse many times is to experience shame and guilt.

Regret. This is a close cousin to remorse. When we experience regret, it's usually because we've chosen to meditate on bad choices and actions from our past. "Why was I put on the earth anyway?" Or "Why did this happen to me?" Or even, "Why did I have to go through what I've been through?" If those are lingering questions in your mind, it may be because you still have shame on your life.

Self-Reproach. This can be the result of experiencing shame. It can also be the activity inside us that leads us to shame.

Dishonor. If you've ever been dishonored, especially if it came from events outside of your control, you experienced shame.

Degradation. This usually is the result of wrong behaviors of people around you that have affected your life. A common example of this is when a child is teased and harassed by other children at school. The degradation confounds them; they don't understand why they are subject to it. Usually there's no good reason; they just are. Sadly, this is a common basis for experiencing shame.

Scandal. Have you ever known someone affected by a scandal? It doesn't matter whether or not he had anything to do with it. To have a family member who committed a criminal act and winds up in prison, that's a scandal. His kids, his spouse, brothers, sisters, mother, father. . . they're all affected by it. It's easy to experience shame because of a scandal.

Again, Mephibosheth's name identified him to himself first. His nurse spoke his name to him, and it proved to him that those outside himself saw him the same way.

Your neighbor, your friends, your uncle, your mom, your dad, your teacher, whoever it was that negatively prophesied into you tried to tell you who you were and what you couldn't do. If you listened to their voices long enough, ultimately you ended up experiencing shame, and it's crippled you.

We can and do have feelings of guilt, but guilt *is* more than a feeling; it describes our legal standing before God without the blood of Christ covering our sins. One aspect of shame is the feelings of shame we experience. But shame *also* describes our response to knowledge of our guilt before God. Our response to guilt without our repentance is to experience shame.

If you don't know the truth about who you are in Christ and what God has made you to be, if you haven't come before the throne of Christ in repentance, you won't understand how to defeat the forces of shame in your life.

If this last part sounds as though there is more than one type of shame we can experience, you're right. Let's continue to examine this in the next chapter.

Chapter 5

WHAT'S THE DIFFERENCE IN SHAME?

Two things need to be known about shame. There are two different ways it can have an entrance into our lives. It can come from an inward response we have to our condition. This happens whenever there are areas of our life we have not repented of. Or it can come from outside of us, because of circumstances beyond our control.

We'll take the first of these types of shame in this chapter and move on to the second in the next chapter.

When it is inward, pride comes into play as a motivating factor. Later on, as we describe how shame manifests in our personality and behavior, this will become very clear. Let's begin with the inward.

THE INWARD NATURE OF SHAME

Remember Adam and Eve? Right there on the first pages of your Bible, God begins the story of creation. Look at an important part of the first reference to Adam and Eve together:

And they were both naked, the man and his wife, and were not ashamed. Genesis 2:25 NKJV

Here they were, new creations in the new creation. Naked, but not ashamed. They had no shame. All too soon that would change.

They were in the garden with every living thing around them. The two trees were there, and a snake.

We know the story. Eve, deceived by a lie of the serpent, ate from the wrong tree. Then she had Adam eat from it also. The only thing in creation they were told to not touch, they did. Suddenly, God comes by. . .

And they heard the sound of the Lord God walking in the garden in the cool of the day, and Adam and his wife hid themselves from the presence of the Lord God among the trees of the garden.

Then the Lord God called to Adam and said to him, "Where are you?"

So he said, "I heard your voice in the garden, and I was afraid because I was naked; and I hid myself." Genesis 3:8-10 NKJV

They went from a condition of no shame, not even a concept of what shame was, to absolute shame. Really, it happened in two stages. Back up a step to the prior verses.

So when the woman saw that the tree was good for food, that it was pleasant to the eyes, and a tree desirable to make one wise, she took of its fruit and ate. She also gave to her husband with her, and he ate.

Then the eyes of both of them were opened, and they knew that they were naked; and they sewed fig leaves together and made themselves coverings. Genesis 3:6-7 NKJV

They *knew;* even before God came along, *they knew something was wrong.* Their first reaction was to create a covering for each other. In their shame, they had to "hide" from each other by sewing fig leaves together. They responded to their awareness of disobedience by experiencing shame.

That led to their second reaction. God came along. Anyone think God didn't know what had just happened? Sure He did. Then why did He come along? He's looking for their response. They responded in shame and hid themselves.

First it's a matter of concealing themselves from each other (remember they're husband and wife), taking leaves to cover themselves. Think about this: they are the only two people on the entire planet, they're married, and they decided to conceal themselves from each other.

Then God showed up and it got worse. Look back at verse 8: *"They hid themselves from the presence of the Lord."*

When our response to our condition is shame, we first hide from each other, then attempt to hide from God. We hide ourselves from the presence of the Lord. It never works, but it's what a person does who is motivated by shame.

But the people wouldn't listen to Samuel. "No," they said. "We will have a king to rule us! Then we'll be just like all the other nations. Our king will rule us and lead us and fight our battles."

Samuel took in what they said and rehearsed it with God. God told Samuel, "Do what they say. Make them a king."

Then Samuel dismissed the men of Israel: "Go home, each of you to your own city." 1 Samuel 8:19-22 The Message Bible

Before it even began with Saul, it started with the people of Israel. Pride was driving them to want a king. They wanted a king they could boast about.

God will give you what you ask for, even if it's not the best thing for you to have. They asked for a king, and God granted them their request.

God chose Saul to become king. He looked right, he came from the right kind of family, and his dad was well off. (Whatever word they use for him in your Bible, it means he's wealthy.) He just seemed like the right kind of guy to fit the part of king of Israel.

But something's wrong with their new king. He went and told Samuel:

> *Saul answered, "I'm only a Benjaminite, from the smallest of Israel's tribes, and from the most insignificant clan in the tribe at that. Why are you talking to me like this?"*
> 1 Samuel 9:21 The Message Bible

In chapter one, we referred to this verse and Saul's question to Samuel. The question reveals his heart.

Adam and Eve's first sin was being self-centered. It was their desire to pridefully satisfy their own desire, not God's command. Their self-centered response to their disobedience was shame.

Pride and shame are fraternal twins. They do not look alike; they were born one right after the other. Pride was the firstborn, and then came its brother, shame.

This is the shame Saul chose to experience. In the face of his present condition, which was about as good as it could get (his dad's rich, he's good looking and strong), he chose shame. This springs out of pride, because it was a self-centered response to the call on his life. His shame was prideful because it allowed him to keep his focus on himself.

Saul's reign as Israel's first king was fraught with his continuing encounters with his own pride. It's what lead him into disobedience and failure as king.

THE STRONGHOLDS OF PRIDE AND SHAME: TOOLS OF THE SELF-CENTERED SOUL

Strongholds of pride and shame keep us wandering aimlessly through a desert of unrest, leading us into confusion, anxiety, depression and despair.

Let me offer a few insights into these strongholds.

Pride is an amazingly effective way for us to fashion little gods for ourselves.

With pride we promote ourselves. With shame we demote ourselves. Both increase self-centeredness.

Pride provides a focus on self-gratification. Then, having been gratified, pride is justified. Therefore, pride is the cause and defender of selfishness.

Pride is that part of our unredeemed self that believes personal performance can overcome our unpleasant feelings of shame.

Shame tells us, "You're right; Jesus did die for me, but don't you still feel ashamed?" Then pride comes right back up, saying, "Since you do feel ashamed, you've got to rely on what you have done, what you are now doing, and what you're able to do so you can feel acceptable to yourself."

Shame will justify its self-centeredness by promoting self's victim status.

Shame is a thief; it steals life's treasures from us. Pride, in its selfishness, buries that treasure where only selfish pride can find it.

The rich may take pride in their riches, and the poor may be ashamed of their condition, but each is only a form of vanity. They are both mirrors used to turn the focus onto self.

Pride hopes someone is watching. Shame is careful to know who is looking. Both take self into the bondage of other's opinions.

Pride may give false hope. But shame gives false hopelessness.

Going back to Saul and David, some would then ask, "Well, what's the difference between Saul's call to be king and David's response to the same call?"

Glad you asked. . .

David trusted God. He didn't look to the inward impulses that had to have been inside him. God called, Samuel showed up at his home, and he accepted the anointing. David's life and reign was one of trust in God. Even after events when he sinned, he turned and repented. He did this because of his trust in God.

Trusting God is central to our recovery and deliverance from shame.

There is another reason we might experience shame. Outside forces and conditions beyond our control can induce shame into our life. That's what we will look at next.

Chapter 6

THE OTHER TYPE OF SHAME

In the last chapter we discovered one of the ways shame can enter our life and the relationship pride has with that shame. There is another type of shame, and the influence it has on our life can come from many sources.

THE OUTWARD NATURE OF SHAME

Shame can enter our lives from events and situations beyond our control.

Mephibosheth's condition is an example of that. As we've found in Scripture, he couldn't have controlled the fall he took when he was five years old. Nothing could have prepared him for that kind of life experience. There's no way he could have known, as a child, how to handle that. His own father, Jonathan, had been killed in battle along with Saul. His dad wasn't there.

Our question is, what are the outside forces that can cause us to experience shame? How does this type of shame develop?

SHAME IS POSSIBLE
WHEN FEAR SURROUNDS YOUR LIFE.

Have you ever seen the old movie made from John Steinbeck's novel, *"The Grapes of Wrath?"*

The beginning of the film portrays 1930's depression era life in Oklahoma, what they used to call the "dust bowl." People were going out of their minds, they were so poor. Poverty without hope. The fear that poverty created in the hearts of people was more than they could stand up under. That drove a generation of people into shame.

When fear surrounds your life, when there is no way to run away from fearful conditions, when an atmosphere of fear prevails, shame has an entrance into a person's heart. It sets in motion the ability for someone to receive shame. Fear is the seed in the soil of your heart from which shame will spring up.

SHAME IS POSSIBLE
WHEN YOU'RE RUNNING BECAUSE OF WHO YOU ARE.

Go back to the verse about Mephibosheth in 2 Samuel 4:4: *"His nurse picked him up and ran. . ."* Mephibosheth's nurse was running for her (and his) life, because this little boy was the grandson of King Saul. He had inherited the relationship to the king, and now that was what was putting him in danger.

SHAME IS POSSIBLE
WHEN THOSE WHO SURROUND YOU
ARE SUPPOSED TO CARRY YOU, BUT DROP YOU.

Let's look at the rest of that verse in 2 Samuel 4:4 *"but in her hurry to get away, she fell, and the boy was maimed."* They were supposed to carry you, but they dropped you. The people around you, who were supposed to protect you, didn't. You were supposed to be safe, but someone failed you, and you weren't. You got injured or maimed, and the imprint of that experience has left an open avenue for shame to enter your life.

SHAME IS POSSIBLE
WHEN THERE'S BEEN A PERSONAL BETRAYAL.

This is closely related to the previous issue, but can have other origins. Find anyone who was molested by a family member when he/she was young. You'll find someone who is still dealing with shame. It wasn't his/her fault. He/she didn't have any control over it, but he/she is the one who suffers with shame.

A much more common problem where all too many suffer betrayal is when there is a divorce. Nothing shows the impact of betrayal more than when one spouse turns against the other and creates the conditions leading to the breakup of a marriage.

Divorce is internalized as a life failure and betrayal. Most of the time, the injured party in the divorce carries the shame, even though he/she had little or nothing to do with the problem.

This creates future problems for shame coming in on the children of a divorced couple. The betrayal becomes the event that opens the inward places of a person's heart to receive shame.

SHAME IS POSSIBLE
WHEN YOUR NAME EXPLAINS YOUR CONDITION.

He wasn't just Jonathan's son Mephibosheth. He was Jonathan's son Mephibosheth, who was crippled in both feet.

Go through the classrooms of the closest elementary school. You will come across those classrooms set aside for the "special needs" students.

Even a few minutes visiting these children can bring an adult to tears. These kids have developmental disabilities, physical disabilities, mental and emotional disabilities that keep them separated from the rest of the student population.

They don't interact with the other children outside of their own classroom. When the other students hear the name of one of these kids, they immediately know who he/she is and associate a world of negative images with that child.

Shame becomes a persistent issue that these children have to battle against throughout their childhood and adolescence.

SHAME IS POSSIBLE
WHEN EMBARRASSMENT DOMINATES YOUR PRESENCE.

David said, "I will show kindness to Hanun son of Nahash, because his father showed kindness to me." And David sent messengers to comfort him concerning his father's death. So the servants of David came into the land of the Ammonites to comfort Hanum.

But the princes of the Ammonites said Hanum, "Do you think that David has sent comforters to you because he honors your father? Have his servants not come to you to search, to overthrow, and to spy out the land?"

Therefore Hanum took David's servants, shaved them, cut off their garments in the middle near their buttocks, and sent them away.

When David was told how the men were served, he sent to meet them; for they were greatly shamed and embarrassed. The king said, "Stay in Jericho until your beards are grown, then return." 1 Chronicles 19:2-5 The Amplified Bible

The servants of David were out doing the king's business and bidding. They had come to offer friendship and comfort to the surviving son of a neighboring king who had just died. They were met with suspicion by the new king, who had taken his father's throne.

The actions of this new young king were calculated to bring embarrassment and humiliation onto these servants. This event was beyond their control and against their will. This embarrassment caused a condition that was shameful to them. They were experiencing shame because of the embarrassment brought upon them.

David commanded them, *"Stay in Jericho until your beards are grown, then return."* This type of shame keeps a person isolated and distant from even their closest friends and family.

SHAME IS POSSIBLE
WHEN YOUR CONDITION SPEAKS LOUDER THAN YOUR
POSITION OR YOUR PERSON.

God didn't create Mephibosheth to be the man who was lame in both feet; that was not His intention. But sometimes your condition dominates your person.

Until you find your true self in God, and the very person of God residing inside of you, you'll never understand the full weight of what God has for you. You'll always see yourself in the light of, "I was born on the wrong side of the tracks, " or something like that. Forget about what side of the tracks you might have come from, and come to Jesus.

SHAME IS POSSIBLE
WHEN DISGRACE BECOMES A STATE OF MIND.

Please look at the following as an example not only of this point, but also of the last few points.

We've all seen them, usually downtown around the courthouse, sometimes by the entrance and exit ramps of major highways and freeways. They're always there. Usually they have a home-made sign on a piece of cardboard. It's got something on it like, "Will Work For Food" or "Please Help."

The stories they tell are different, but alike in many ways. They had a good job, a family, a home. The basic things in their life were going well. Then it happened. The family broke up, and the job was lost. Something hit hard, and it was beyond their ability to handle. The fabric of their life got torn apart.

All of a sudden, they couldn't provide for their kids or their wife. The good home they had went away. The cars went, too. No way to afford a car to get around in.

What seemed like a small loss really sends them over the edge. They lose their telephone service. When the phone is gone, the ability to seek and pursue another job gets lost also. Sure, they can walk down to apply for a job, but with no way for an employer to call them back, they're sunk. With no phone to call up the businesses that have "help wanted" ads in the paper, no car to drive to the businesses that advertised for help, they've lost the chance to pursue that next job before they even start.

They didn't have a backup. Like most people, they lived a good life, but it's paycheck to paycheck. Just enough is coming in to cover basic necessities. No one was there to turn to for help. Maybe the parents had long since passed away. Maybe the brothers or sisters didn't care, didn't want to be bothered.

The shock and dismay of their condition does a number on their mind. Hope doesn't even seem like an option. They are disgraced by the condition they are in.

Usually, they really do want to pull things back together...get back together with their wife; get the kids back with them. By the time things get this low and this bad in their life, they are living life out in a perpetual state of shock and dismay. They are disgraced by the condition of their life. Life becomes a constant experience of shame.

By the time they've gone wandering out in the city parks, on the highways, and behind the warehouses, their minds have become so unraveled that they no longer know how to receive encouragement and hope. No wonder when some of the homeless get in their homeless state, it takes years to get their minds healed again. The shame runs so deep, the possibility of recovery never looks real to them.

SHAME IS POSSIBLE
WHEN PAINFUL FEELINGS OF YOUR PAST
HOLD YOU CAPTIVE.

Here's a true story; doesn't matter whose story it is though. It happens so often.

I know a guy who wanted to work with the camera crews on motion picture productions out in Hollywood. He carried this dream for twenty, maybe thirty years. Finally he got a chance to get a job in Los Angeles, working at a camera shop in Hollywood. It looked good; it was the right place to run into some of the right people. Problem was, just as some of the best contacts had already been made, the job was lost.

Los Angeles is an expensive place to live. It's incredibly so when there's no job and no money coming in. The concerns for income took priority over any hope of pursuing the hope and dreams held for so long. After about a year and a half of struggling, the family intervened and retrieved the young man back to his hometown.

Back home (home could be anyplace), it's just not where the hope was, and despair set in. The disappointment of the missed opportunities was revisited daily. The feelings of failure and disappointment held the man's heart captive. Those feelings, when internalized, develop into a profound sense of shame. It's as though life stops. There's no place to progress to, because the hope held close in the heart for so many years is missed.

Some people are so held captive to their past, they have no hope for a future. They wind up not even wanting help. They don't like where they're at today but are unwilling to change anything for their future.

No doubt there's a hope and future that were missed. But to enter into the hope and future God offers (where it's real), there has to be a willingness to change.

SHAME IS POSSIBLE
WHEN YOUR FAMILY'S REPUTATION
NEGATIVELY PRECEDES YOU.

Remember the beginning of the last chapter? What was going on when Adam and Eve sinned and ate of the wrong tree? That's what comes up here.

The old pop song goes, "Love the one you're with," but that doesn't always mean you're proud of them. Most every family has a skeleton or two in the closet they'd rather no one knew about. Having those things known is a negative reflection on the entire family. Sometimes the issues are very serious and would be more than just a slight embarrassment to a family.

Maybe it's a father who had a problem with lust, so much so that he wound up getting arrested for a behavior that was acted out. Maybe it's a son or daughter who had a problem with drugs. Sometimes, it's that precious daughter who experiences a pregnancy while in high school. These are just some of the most obvious things that might cause a negative reputation for an entire family.

Unfortunately, most of the time, the rest of the family is *ashamed* of whatever situation it is and wants it to stay hidden. It's the same response Adam and Eve had in the garden. Let's hide it, keep it hidden. Shame rears its ugly head because pride says, *"Nobody can see this!"*

SHAME IS POSSIBLE
WHEN YOU'RE CONNECTED TO SOMEONE
WHO'S UNDER THE JUDGMENT HAND OF GOD.

Mephibosheth was in Lo Debar, the dry place. He was hiding from King David. He didn't want to be seen, suffering from double shame. He was crippled in both feet, but also he was from the house of Saul.

His grandfather was the one who disobeyed God, tried to kill God's anointed David, and couldn't get a word from God on his own, so he sent the witch to call up Samuel. Saul was strong in himself and not in God. Saul's the one who lost his mind.

If you're not careful, the one you're connected to who's being judged by God can bring shame on your life.

Shame is a condition. The word shame in Hebrew, "bosheth," means an "idol." It can mean ashamed and confused, but one of the specific things it means is, an idol.

Shame can be such a dominating experience in your life that it controls your life. It controls your personality, your behavior, how you live out your entire life. We're going to delve into the behaviors based on shame in the next chapter.

But know this right now: the power of God is coming. The hand of God is here with us right now to restore broken dreams and broken relationships. The hand of the Lord is here right now to navigate us through overwhelming situations.

God wants to do a "walk through" into our entire life to heal and restore, to cover with the blood of Christ. His desire is to have us understand who we really are in Christ, not what has been spoken over us that brought us into shame.

Meditate on the promise given in this Scripture:

Zephaniah 3: 14-20

"Sing, O daughter of Zion! Shout, O Israel!
Be glad and rejoice with all you heart,
O daughter of Jerusalem!

The Lord has taken away your judgments. He has cast out
your enemy. The King of Israel, the Lord, is in your midst; you
shall see disaster no more.

In that day it shall be said to Jerusalem: "Do not fear;
Zion, let not your hands be weak.

The Lord your God in your midst, The Mighty One, will
save; He will rejoice over you with gladness,
He will quiet you in His love,
He will rejoice over you with singing.

I will gather those who sorrow
over the appointed assembly, who are among you, to whom
its reproach is a burden. Behold, at that time I will deal with all
who afflict you;

I will save the lame, and gather those who were driven out; I
will appoint them for praise and fame in every land where they
were put to shame.

At that time I will bring you back, even at the time I gather
you; for I will give you fame and praise among
all the peoples of the earth, when I return your captives
before your eyes, says the Lord."
NKJV

That scripture deals with a nation facing judgment because of their sinfulness. God said through the prophet Zephaniah, "When it's all through, anyone who's brought shame on you will have to face your fame. When I'm through dealing with you, you'll be a trophy of my grace to be put on display."

The word *praise* actually means to be put on display. It's going to be an outward thing. Turn to Jesus; repent of those things on the inside that turned you to shame. Turn to Jesus; He will help you overcome every lie of the devil spoken over your life.

God said that He's going to take you from shame to fame. He'll put you up as a testimony, as a witness, and you'll be able to say, "I don't know how I did it; they told me I couldn't, I shouldn't, but here I am by the grace of God and the blood of Christ. I want to give God praise; look what the Lord has done for me!"

Chapter 7

THE MARKS AND BEHAVIORS OF SHAME

It is my sincere hope that as you read from the third chapter of Zephaniah, you will begin to understand how much God desires your freedom from shame.

God wants us free from the tyranny of shame over our lives. My hope as we go on is that you would be able to pull the veil away from your eyes a little bit and see the freedom ahead.

Much of what I'm presenting here is written grammatically in the third person, distancing it from us a little bit. I'm trying not to make any assumptions about what your condition is, but I have to guess that if you're reading this book, if you've read this far, there are issues you want to know about.

Up to now we've shown how shame can come on us and in us, how our conditions and choices determine our experience of shame.

Now we need to learn how our personality and behavior are shaped by the shame resident in our lives.

CHARACTERISTICS OF THOSE DRIVEN BY SHAME

When shame is present in someone's life, it has a profound affect on one's behavior and personality. He/she becomes driven by guilt, fear, and an overwhelming desire to please others.

Since these people are driven by these motivations, they in turn act upon the world the way shame forces them to see it. Because of this, they usually use guilt, fear and the careful withholding of approval as tools to manipulate other people.

WHEN SHAME IS PRESENT, THERE IS LOW SELF-ESTEEM.

When people are contending with shame in their life, they cannot honor and respect themselves or others. They are trapped by their own self-consciousness, sense of inadequacy, and their defense mechanisms, which shield them from their own hypersensitive self-judgments.

WHEN SHAME IS PRESENT, THERE IS A DISTORTED VIEW OF OTHERS.

When shame is present, people find themselves dealing with anger at levels they dare not admit to. Many times that anger frightens even them. They project these feelings outside of themselves.

What's typical is they make themselves victims by viewing others as angry, mean, controlling, judgmental, or hostile.

Their victim status needs to be maintained, so their feelings that others are hostile or unfair tend to remain unchanged also. In fact, they bristle when challenged that their perspective of those they view with these tendencies is wrong.

WHEN SHAME IS PRESENT,
THERE IS A DISTORTED VIEW OF SELF.

Whether it's conscious or unconscious, they're unable to deal with the fact that they too can and do make mistakes. When shame is present, they resort to denials and distortions about what their behavior is.

We've all seen people who are "hard on themselves" or who see themselves as superior to others. They tend to exaggerate their good behaviors and performance, while making little if any note of their failures.

The world outside of themselves may not recognize their little white lies. Moreover, they may not be able to recognize their self-deception, either.

What can start as a "little white lie" can blossom into a bigger and bigger "fish tale" that gets larger with every telling. People with this level of shame are so captivated by their grandiose image of themselves that in their mind, they wonder how anyone can do without them.

WHEN SHAME IS PRESENT,
A PERSON IS MOTIVATED BY FEAR.

Perhaps nothing keeps us in bondage the way fear does. The greater the fear, the greater the need for some way to block or censor our mind from those fears. We are held in bondage to our fears, never able to become free from them. We become ever more sensitive to those things we fear. As that sensitivity escalates, we become more "touchy," more self-defensive and quick to respond when our fears are aroused.

WHEN SHAME IS PRESENT,
THE MORE JUDGMENTAL A PERSON BECOMES.

Closely related to a person's fear motivations is the tendency for a shame-based person to pigeon-hole other people and their behaviors into rigid categories. Everything is black and white; there's never any gray area about another person's behavior. Judgments always come down to yes or no, good or bad, safe or unsafe. People who act out of shame have an "all or nothing" attitude. When discouragement or frustration arises, there's the impulse to just "throw the baby out with the bath water."

WHEN SHAME IS PRESENT,
SELF-CRITICISM IS HEIGHTENED.

Those who are subjected to a shame-based person's judgment may experience guilt. But the person dishing it out is judging him or herself with even less mercy, being more critical, and is more unfair to himself than to anyone else.

Shame has become his teacher. It has taught him that he is either good or bad, saint or sinner, perfect or failure, competent or incompetent. . . worst of all, whether or not he is either worthy of love or unworthy of love. He dictates to himself whether or not he is worthy of Christ's love and His atonement for his sins.

WHEN SHAME IS PRESENT,
THERE IS A FEAR OF ABANDONMENT.

To the shame-based person, abandonment is a fate worse than death. It has to be avoided at all costs. The response to this fear is to become a people-pleaser. He is driven into perfectionism. He lives life by giving in, over-extending himself to find love. He also exhibits the opposite behavior by putting up rigid boundaries to *avoid relationships* and thus abandonment.

WHEN SHAME IS PRESENT, THERE IS A PROFOUND SENSE OF LONELINESS.

The loneliness of a shame-based person results in his continual attempts to avoid relationships and remain detached.

It's a circular behavior; if he can avoid relationships, he can avoid being abandoned. But that only serves to drive him further into loneliness. He becomes detached and develops a preference for isolation from others.

That isolation is accomplished in three primary ways:

(1)   Physical withdrawal
(2)   Emotional withdrawal
(3)   Putting on a very guarded "life of the party" façade.

This last tool of isolation and detachment develops into such a practiced behavior it's important to look at it in greater detail.

THE SHAME-BASED FAÇADE

This is the most skilled and deceptive response of a shame-based personality. It is such a deceptive activity, the person is unaware of his or her own behavior.

He exhibits a lively, enjoyable conversation that (unknown to others) *is not* intended to befriend anyone or initiate or deepen relationships. Instead, the façade is intended to keep the conversation in his control. This accomplishes at least seven objectives.

First, it lets him control the topic of conversation.

Second, it lets him control the emotional distance and tone of conversation.

Third, it helps him feel good about himself and receive positive regard from others.

Fourth, it prevents him from having to get involved in others' conversations at anything more than a shallow level.

Fifth, used effectively, it helps prevent any unexpected intrusion.

Sixth, it puts the environment securely in his control, and among other things,

Seventh, it gives him a sense of friendly positive affirmation without having to get involved with a more intimate friendship.

There are other variations of this "social" façade. Some shame-based individuals ramble incessantly, never giving others a chance to speak. Whatever they do, the loneliness still remains. As long as they are dominated by shame, they will seek to shut out any awareness of their loneliness, even if that means repressing this anxious awareness deep inside their unconscious mind.

MARKS OF A SHAME-BASED PERSONALITY

How can we know and understand if our own personality and behaviors are expressions of shame? What follows is a self-review to assist you in your own understanding. Don't worry; there's no scoring here, just some things for you to reflect on and take to the Lord. Take your time, and be sensitive to the Holy Spirit as you read this.

1. You already know that you've isolated yourself from others, particularly those you perceive to be in authority (such as pastors, teachers, doctors). You mistrust anyone who would come alongside to help and support you.

2. You're aware of your own tendency to seek others' approval. You feel confusion deep inside. You don't seem to have much of a sense of personal identity. Your need for approval compromises your pursuit of the call of God on your life.

3. You're overly sensitive to criticism. You'll do anything to avoid criticism. When you are criticized, you: (a) become angry and bitter at the source of the criticism, (b) become passive, fearful, and accommodating to avoid any criticism, (c) distance yourself from others and remain aloof, (d) become a perfectionist, compulsively driven to control anyone who might criticize you.

4. You find you are most comfortable with others who share compulsive personalities. This is where the infamous "CD" phrase gets introduced – you discover you're involved in Co-Dependent relationships. These are the relationships you gravitate to for security.

5. It's easier to deal with others' problems rather than your own. By focusing on the problems of others, you divert yourself from confronting your own shame-based issues.

6. You have feelings of guilt whenever you stand up for yourself. You give in so others will like you. If there's a conflict, you compromise instead of standing up for yourself. Here's the tough part: it's hard for you to pursue your long-term God-given vision for your life whenever that vision is challenged and conflicts arise.

7. You experience life as a *victim*. You see yourself as a victim because of what *others* have done to you. You think they're out to get you, and you want to lash out at them. You're in denial about your own responsibility for your own feelings. This behavior can be a major stumbling block to repentance, because it's always someone else's fault, never your own.

8. If you think you haven't done something absolutely perfectly, you're a failure. You really believe that that's how everyone else sees you. Your attitude is, "Anyone could have done it better."

9. You can't express your feelings to anyone. Only in your private inner self do you have any experience of feelings at all. In fact, you may have lost the ability to feel or express any feelings at all, with this possible exception: when pushed, you will express anger. It's almost always your only release.

10. You don't seek close, personal relationships where you can share your deepest feelings.

11. Nonetheless, you have a dependent personality. This comes out of your fear of abandonment and rejection and your need for approval. You will do anything for others.

12. If you spend a lot of time around others who are shame-based and controlling, you begin to take on their negative attitudes and behaviors.

13. You react to life instead of initiating your own purposes and decisions in life. You avoid important decisions. Anything to maintain the *status quo*. However, you do work hard to maintain the appearance of busyness and confidence.

There's a way out of this jungle, and that's why you've got this book in your hands. Don't faint yet; God's here and is ready to heal and redeem. Let's go to the next chapter for some answers.

Note: This chapter is largely taken from two on-line postings written by the Rev. Thomas F. Fischer, M.Div., M.S.A. "Sixteen Marks of a Shame-Based Ministry" and "Eight Characteristics of a Shame-Based Ministry" and are copyrighted ©1997-2006 Ministry Health LLC with All Rights Reserved. These postings are available for viewing at the website http://www.ministryhealth.net

Chapter 8

RECOVERY FROM SHAME

Shame for some is obvious; it's a condition they are familiar with and acknowledge. For others, it's an unknown condition. Behaviors and conditions will persist and trouble them for a lifetime. They know something's wrong, but they don't know why. The root problem is unknown. There's been no way to connect the dots.

We're trying to do just that. Let's get the connections made and move forward to hope and recovery. God's promised a full, joyful life in Christ. Embrace those promises and come into healing.

There's an old saying concerning Scripture that, "The New (Testament) is hidden in the Old, and the Old (Testament) is revealed in the New." It's what some describe as "types and shadows."

Saul and his disobedience, David and his covenant with Jonathan, Mephibosheth and his elevation to eat at the table of King David are all true events. Their place in Scripture is a marker for us to see and understand how God can and does save, redeem, and transform us today.

In the plan of God, with the death and resurrection of Jesus, it is a finished work. It's up to us today to come to Christ, repent of our sin and our sinful ways, accept His forgiveness, and by faith in Him receive the inheritance planned for us from the beginning of time.

By now we know what shame is, how it gets started, how it gets in us, how it can come on us. We've also learned the behaviors and traits that invade our personality when shame is in our life.

THE WAYS THAT GOD RESTORES FROM SHAME

I want to show you the ways that God will redeem and restore a life plagued by shame. Again, look back to David and see his activity with Mephibosheth as a "type" or "model" of God's restoration out of shame.

King David didn't lose a minute. He sent and got him from the home of Makir, son of Ammiel, in Lo Debar.

When Mephibosheth, son of Jonathan (who was the son of Saul), came before David, he bowed deeply, abasing himself, honoring David.

David spoke his name: "Mephibosheth."

"Yes sir?"

"Don't be frightened," said David, "I'd like to do something special for you in memory of your father Jonathan. To begin with, I'm returning to you all the properties of your grandfather Saul. Furthermore, from now on you'll take all your meals at my table."

Shuffling and stammering, not looking him in the eye, Mephibosheth said, "Who am I that you pay attention to a stray dog like me?"

David then called in Ziba, Saul's right-hand man, and told him, "Everything that belonged to Saul and his family, I've handed over to your master's grandson. You and your son and your servants will work his land and bring in the produce, provisions for your master's grandson. Mephibosheth himself, your master's grandson, from now on will take all his meals at my table." Ziba had fifteen sons and twenty servants.

"All that my master the king has ordered his servant," answered Ziba, *"your servant will surely do."*

And Mephibosheth ate at David's table, just like one of the royal family. Mephibosheth also had a small son named Mica. All who were part of Ziba's household were now the servants of Mephibosheth.

Mephibosheth lived in Jerusalem, taking all his meals at the king's table. He was lame in both feet.
2 Samuel 9:5-13 The Message Bible

1. GOD BRINGS YOU OUT OF DRY PLACES.

O God, you are my God;
Early will I seek You;
My soul thirsts for You;
My flesh longs for You
In a dry and thirsty land
Where there is no water.
Psalms 63:1 NKJV

David brought Mephibosheth up from Lo Debar, where he was living. "Lo Debar" means "dry places." There's nothing worse than being in a dry place or situation. You can actually be personally dry and not be in a dry place, which seems to indicate that you can be in a great church and still be dry.

Then again, you can be seeking and be in a dry place. It means you're in a dry condition. It doesn't feel like you can really get your prayers answered. You're praying because you know you should pray, but you're just hitting a ceiling. Nothing seems to be moving. You're afraid something won't happen.

The King called for Mephibosheth and said to get him out of Lo Debar; he can't live there; he'll die there.

2. GOD REASSIGNS YOUR NAME.

It's interesting. As we learned several chapters back, Mephibosheth means "breathing shame." Research it a bit more and you discover that names can have more than one meaning. It's fascinating, because in Hebrew it also means "dispeller of shame."

In Hebrew thought, when they changed the name, it was because of an inward change of nature. If you can be changed on the inside, your name must represent who you are. In Hebrew, you didn't get named Jim just because your uncle was named Jim. It wasn't just a family tradition.

Earlier, when we learned about how significant the meanings of names are, we found that names are a prophecy about a person.

God came to Abram, which means "exalted father," and named him Abraham, which means "father of great multitudes." He changed Sarai, which means "my princess," to be Sarah, which means "a princess for the people." He took the name, Jacob, which means "trickster," and changed it to Israel, which means "prince of God." He took Simon, which means "pebble," and changed his name to Peter, which means "stone." God wants to change your identity.

3. GOD REMOVES FEAR FROM YOUR LIFE.

2 Samuel 9:7 says, *"Don't be afraid."* Fear is paralyzing. Remember growing up, you probably watched the wrong movie before you went to bed, then when you went to bed and you woke up with a nightmare, you were paralyzed by fear.

We think of fear as an emotion. It can be that. Really, it's a spirit.

For God has not given us a spirit of fear, but of power and of love and of a sound mind. 2 Timothy 1:7 NKJV

God's given you the ability to think with a right mind, but when fear grips you, it hinders you. So God removes fear from your life.

David spoke, *"Mephibosheth, don't be afraid, I'm the king; I remove fear from you right now."*

4. GOD HEALS WITH KINDNESS.

Over the years, you've probably heard of some of the old time preachers who were known as "hell-fire and brimstone" preachers. Some are still around, and some of you grew up with a pastor who preached like that.

When that's the case, our early ideas of who God is are molded into a concept of an angry God. It's hard to handle that and also know how to accept that it's the same God referred to in John 3:16, *"For God so loved the world. . ."*

Truth is, God is reaching out to you, to love you into His kingdom. He longs and desires to get you out of the situations you're in, out of what's been holding you back and hemming you in. God wants to show you His kindness.

Let's go to a few earlier verses in the Bible, from the book of Exodus, as Moses talks to God on Mount Sinai:

And he (Moses) said, "Please, show me your glory." Then He (God) said, "I will make all My goodness pass before you and I will proclaim the name of the Lord before you. I will be gracious

to whom I will be gracious, and I will have compassion on whom I will have compassion." Exodus 33:18-19 NKJV

And the Lord passed before him and proclaimed, "The Lord, the Lord God, merciful and gracious, longsuffering, and abounding in goodness and truth, keeping mercy for thousands, forgiving iniquity and transgression and sin, by no means clearing the guilty, visiting the iniquity of the fathers upon the children and the children's children to the third and fourth generation." Exodus 34:6-7 NKJV

If, while reading this book, you were to walk away not learning one other thing about the Lord, please learn this;

That is how God wants to be known by us! It is, as I've heard it taught, **God's DNA.** It's God's core nature. It's the most fundamental revelation of who God is from the beginning of creation.

So, to paraphrase how it was expressed in Scripture, David, when he looked at Mephibosheth, said, *"I will surely show you kindness for the sake of your father Jonathan. I didn't bring you here because you're under the judgment of your grandfather, Saul. You're here because of the covenant with Jonathan, and now as a result of that, I want to show you some kindness."*

5. *GOD RESTORES BACK WHAT THE ENEMY STOLE.*

Go back into 1 Samuel 30. The Amalekites had invaded the South, gone into a city, Ziklag, and burned it, and had taken captive David's wives. David sought the Lord.

So David inquired of the Lord, saying, "Shall I pursue this troop? Shall I overtake them?" And He answered him, "Pursue, for you shall surely overtake them and without fail recover all." 1 Samuel 30:8 NKJV

And David attacked them from twilight until the evening of the next day. Not a man of them escaped, except four hundred young men who rode on camels and fled. So David recovered all that the Amalekites had carried away, and David rescued his two wives. 1 Samuel 30:17-18 NKJV

When God heals and redeems, He restores.

Thank God for His gift to you of repentance, for the blood of Jesus Christ that washes you and restores your soul, and revives your spirit. He's going to recover everything the enemy stole from your life.

6. GOD PUTS YOU IN PLACES OF AUTHORITY.

God places you in seats of authority when He lifts shame off your life. He's going to put you in a position of authority.

The Scripture says, *"You will always eat at my table."* Not everybody ate at the king's table.

But God is so rich in mercy, and He loved us so very much, that even while we were dead because of our sins, He gave us life when He raised Christ from the dead. (It is only by God's special favor that you have been saved!) For He raised us from the dead along with Christ, and we are seated with Him in the heavenly realms-all because we are one with Christ Jesus. Ephesians 2:4-6 NLT

Some people don't know where they're seated. They feel as if they're seated at their house, or at a low place on their job. It hasn't entered their minds yet where Christ has seated them.

7. *GOD PROVIDES HELP.*

David then called in Ziba, Saul's right-hand man, and told him, "Everything that belonged to Saul and his family, I've handed over to your master's grandson. You and your sons and your servants will work his land and bring in the produce, provisions for your master's grandson. Mephibosheth himself, your master's grandson, from now on will take all his meals at my table." Ziba had fifteen sons and twenty servants.
2 Samuel 9:9-10 The Message Bible

They weren't farming the land for the crops to feed Mephibosheth, because he was at the king's table. Why would you eat what was brought in from the field when the meal is already prepared? He was saying, in effect, *"I'll give you help, so that everything is going to be provided for."*

Chances are that Mephibosheth was so low in his mind and his spirit that he didn't realize he had help. It didn't cross his mind. Evidently, Ziba was just out there doing his own thing. Who knows who was farming the land? It doesn't indicate where Ziba was.

Aren't you glad you serve a God named Jehovah Jireh? Don't misunderstand His name; it is not "God who provides." The name means "God who is provider." God's not providing our provision; **He is our provision!**

8. GOD ESTABLISHES A NEW IDENTIFICATION OF ROYALTY.

Mephibosheth ate at the king's table, like one of the king's sons. If you eat at the King's table, you have favor.

The Bible says, "You're a chosen people, a royal priesthood, a holy nation, a people belonging to God. You belong to God." He has called you out of darkness into His marvelous light.

9. GOD ESTABLISHES A NEW GENERATION.

When shame is broken over our life, when we've laid it at the cross of Christ Jesus, the curse of that shame is broken. It stops the transference of those behaviors and personality traits into the next generation. It stops it cold.

Mephibosheth's name changed its meaning. He was the one who was known as "he who breathes shame." Now he is known as "the dispeller of shame." As far as Mephibosheth was concerned, the thing that had been inside of him taking him out (his name) has now brought him in.

10. GOD REMOVES THE SHAME.

There's an old term for when someone who's not responsible for a wrong act, has the blame for it attached to him. He is called a "scapegoat."

That has its origin in the laws given by God to Moses for the nation of Israel, in the book of Leviticus, chapter 16.

When the high priest would go into the Holy of Holies, the inner sanctuary of the tabernacle, he would present the offerings brought by the people (a goat) to the Lord as atonement for their sins. That offering was known as the "sin offering."

But there was another goat that Aaron took from the people.

> *And when he has made an end of atoning for the Holy Place, the tabernacle of meeting, and the altar, he shall bring the live goat; and Aaron shall lay both his hands on the head of the live goat, confess over it all the iniquities of the children of Israel, and all their transgressions, concerning all their sins, putting them on the head of the goat, and shall send it away into the wilderness by the hand of a suitable man. The goat shall bear on itself all their iniquities to an uninhabited land: and he shall release the goat in the wilderness.* Leviticus 16:20-22 NKJV

At the beginning of this chapter, I referred to "New, hidden in the Old; and the Old revealed in the New." This is where we see the clear implication of this.

The blood sacrifice of the goat that Aaron presented to the Lord in the Holy of Holies took care of the legal standing of the people before the Lord. Their legal condition of "guilt" was atoned for by the sacrifice. The sin itself, the actual "thing" that the sin was, its nature, was put upon the goat, which was lead outside the camp into the wilderness.

Christ, when crucified, was not only offering His body up as atonement for our sins, but also changing our legal standing before the throne of God. He was removing the actual thing that the sin was in our life.

This is what He does with our shame. He not only removes our experience of the shame as we repent of it; He takes the shame itself away from our life.

God wants to transition you. He wants to take you from the place that the enemy had you and bring you to the place He has for you. It's time to move from all your limitations and have the shame lifted off your life.

In the next chapter, we will learn practical ways to transition out of shame-based behaviors in our life.

Chapter 9

TRANSFERRING OUT OF SHAME-BASED BEHAVIORS

Nothing is wasted with God. He uses all of our experiences, background, and conditions as instruments in our life to reveal His love, truth, grace, mercy, and forgiveness to us.

When Christ heals us from our shame and guilt, we are delivered from a world of darkness and confusion. Nevertheless, we need to understand the practical directions to walk out from the darkness of shame we have been in bondage to.

What follows are the beginnings of those directions. Our purpose is to engage life in the freedom and liberty we receive as redeemed sons and daughters of the Most High God.

If shame has bound you, if through the pages of this book the Holy Spirit has brought a new understanding to your heart, then follow these directions into freedom from shame.

GOD'S HEART IS TO HAVE YOU LIVE FREE FROM SHAME.

Begin by knowing that God has not shamed you. God will not shame you. It is not His heart for you. God's desire is your freedom. You, as a child of God, are the object of His love. Receive this into your heart and mind right now: Jesus loves you.

If you've believed that somehow, someway, the shame you've experienced had its origin in God's will for you, reject that lie from your life today. The enemy's first tool from the beginning of time has been deception, getting you to somehow lose trust in your Father God. Our responses to those lies were the first seeds of shame inside ourselves. Other things may have provoked shame also. But once it's there, and it's your daily experience, look up and know that God is there with you right now, and He's moving to deliver you *now*.

Our challenge is what it has always been: will we receive God's truth about His love for us? That was our challenge when we first came to know Christ by believing on Him, accepting His forgiveness of our sins, and knowing our spirit was reborn in His likeness.

O Lord, I have come to you for protection; don't let me be put to shame. Rescue me, for you always do what is right. Psalm 31:1 NLT

I am overcome with joy because of your unfailing love, for you have seen my troubles, and you care about the anguish of my soul. Psalm 31:7 NLT

STEPPING OUT OF THE PAST

If you've identified with the behaviors and personality traits that we've shown come from a place of shame, look now for ways to turn around. Remember that the word "repent" means to "turn away from." That's what we're asking you to do now. Turn away, leave that old person behind, and come into freedom.

First, *own up and admit to those areas in your life where you have been motivated by approval.* Approval addiction is much more subtle and deceptive than we think we know about.

Seeking approval is likely one of the single greatest motivations for manipulative personality traits. Life becomes the pursuit of approval, and if the world has to get turned up on its side for that approval to happen, well then, so be it.

Have you ever heard a family member say something like this? *"You guys have no idea how I've sacrificed to keep peace in this family!"* Maybe you've said something like that yourself a few times around the dinner table. Know this: *that is the voice of a master manipulator,* doing anything possible to control relationships and situations to (in his mind) keep peace, as a result, maintaining one's perceived approval from everyone in the family.

That's what approval addiction drives a person into. That person is the one who has to sacrifice, unable to receive the peace God gives. He or she needs to somehow control situations to generate peace out of one's own strength.

As the truth and reality of God's transforming power is embraced, the restless pursuit of that approval is abandoned, and the soul finds rest in the security of Christ's love for us.

Second, recognize that success and failure both occur, and seldom is either final. Don't avoid opportunities that could lead to success in your life. Don't run from the failures, either. Welcome success *and* failure as opportunities for growth and continued spiritual transformation.

Third, have the courage to deal with a "gray" world. Learn to overcome the pain we all deal with as we sort through the complexity of emotions, choices, and behaviors. Life's not an event; it's a process. Mistakes we make are hardly ever final unless we choose to make them final.

We can rejoice, too, when we run into problems and trials, for we know that they are good for us—they help us learn to endure. And endurance develops strength of character in us, and character strengthens our confident expectation of salvation
Romans 5:3-4 NLT

Here's a quotation from Teddy Roosevelt I keep close at hand. It is an encouragement for my tough times and hard decisions. It reminds me to commit to living life. Looking at these last two points, I believe it would be good for you, too.

It is not the critic who counts, not the man who points out how the strong man stumbles, or where the doer of deeds could have done them better. The credit belongs to the man in the arena, whose face is marred by dust and sweat and blood; who strives valiantly. . . who knows the great enthusiasms, the great devotions; who spends himself in a worthy cause; who at the best knows in the end the triumph of high achievement, and who at the worst, if he fails, at least fails while daring greatly, so that his place shall never be with those cold and timid souls who have known neither victory nor defeat.
Teddy Roosevelt, 26th president of the United States

I would strongly encourage you to copy this and put it someplace where you can see it every day.

Fourth, seek the Lord for insight into your problems. Don't avoid the difficult situations God allows into your life. God wants you to grow up. That means you have to learn to master your life, here and now. God is with you *right now* to lead and guide. That's what He's waiting for. . . you calling to Him to speak to you in the details of your life.

Want to enjoy the provisions that God has promised you? Then learn to handle the responsibilities and challenges in your life today. Why are those things there for you to deal with? So you can grow up in Him. Re-read the verse from Romans 3 on the previous page. Father God wants His children to become robust, mature men and women prepared to rule and reign in His Kingdom.

Fifth, stop pretending you have it all together! You don't. *Nobody does.* Quit with the judgmental attitude, the self-righteous behavior. That's your false self. That disguises anger. It leads to an inability to form mature, open and trusting relationships.

If you find yourself behaving so others will think you're virtuous, you're not fooling anyone. That's okay; you're going to have to trust God, and as you do, trust that the people around you want to know the real you, the authentic you. Give your brothers and sisters a chance.

*"It's who you are and the way you live that count before God. Your worship must engage your spirit in the pursuit of truth. That's the kind of people the Father is out looking for: those who are simply and honestly **themselves** before him in their worship. God is sheer being itself—Spirit. Those who worship him must do it out of their very being, their spirits, their true selves, in adoration."* John 4:23-24 The Message Bible

God knows the true you, the one that's way down inside you. That's the person Christ died for and forgave. That's the one He's delivering and making free right now. He wants the real you, that person deep inside, worshiping him. In fact, the only kind of worship He defines as true worship is when that real person inside you shows up before Him in worship.

Sixth, those things deep inside you that you believe are the reasons for your shame. . . accept those things and start to work through them. This may mean that you go through a time of pain.

As you face up to the hidden areas of your heart, you're going to encounter strong anger, bitterness, and resentment inside yourself. This won't be easy. The fact that it's difficult is the evidence of how much it's controlled your life.

Are you willing to be challenged by the reality of your heart's condition? Are you willing to confront the source of the shame you carry? If you are, as you deal with the real issues, deal with the anger and bitterness, you will begin to experience depths of joy in your life you've never known. If you aren't, you will continue to be haunted by shame's influence and control over your life.

Seventh, recognize where you are unable to forgive, and release the hurts and wounds you've suffered. Sometimes the thing that drives us into our shame-based behaviors is the very thing we can't let go of. This, again, is the evidence of how strongly these things are controlling your life.

Go to Jesus and admit to Him that you don't have the ability in your natural self to forgive and release.

> *But those that wait on the Lord*
> *Shall renew their strength;*
> *They shall mount up with wings like eagles,*
> *They shall run and not be weary,*
> *They shall walk and not faint.*
> Isaiah 40:31 NKJV

Look in the margins of a good Bible and you will find that the word "wait" in this verse means to *bind oneself to,* and the phrase "renew their strength" means *to exchange their strength for His strength.* It would be correct to interpret that part of the verse this way: *Those that bind themselves to the Lord shall exchange their strength for His strength.* God gives His ability to you as you lay down your ability. When Christ is your *life,* He gives the freedom to forgive and the ability to respond with love. That's what He's waiting for, and it's what He's offering to you.

Eighth, recognize that you've been viewing the world as a good or bad, black or white, all or nothing experience. Discover the world of options available to you in your life. God wants you free to discover the joy of living your life in Him.

Use caution. As you get free from the shame, you'll begin to discover so many options in life are available that you may experience confusion and get overwhelmed.

Ninth, seek out a more mature brother or sister in the Lord. That may be your pastor. It could be someone you've had a strong, established relationship with. The experience of shame you're carrying in your life didn't happen overnight. These are deeply entrenched patterns that tend to repeat over and over. Find someone who has some experience in this area of counseling. Allow God to direct you to the right person.

Tenth, recognize and accept yourself as a sinful human being, who is forgiven and accepted as a Child of God. You're human; God knows that.

If you're finding hope, encouragement and fresh direction here, that's the work of the Holy Spirit in your life right now. Allow the Holy Spirit full access to the inner recesses of your life. Let the walls around your heart come down.

From Shame to Fame by Gary McIntosh

Note: This chapter is largely taken from an on-line posting written by the Rev. Thomas F. Fischer, M.Div., M.S.A. "Eight Characteristics of a Shame-Based Ministry" and are copyrighted ©1997-2006 Ministry Health LLC with All Rights Reserved. These postings are available for viewing at the website http://www.ministryhealth.net

For further reading see Joan Borysenko, "Guilt is the Lesson, Love is the Teacher" (Warner Books, 1990), Chapter Two, pp. 26 ff and Dennis Wholey's book, "Becoming Your Own Parent (1988)

After the Deliverance

We've looked at how shame and bondage take up residence in our lives, from both the inward responses all of us have, to recognition of sin in our lives, to the outside influences of shame. Next we looked at how shame motivates our attitudes and behaviors and how it affects our personality.

But God wants us free. By the blood of Christ we have God's promises to deliver us from the weight of this. We've looked at how God will release us from the shame and remove it from our life. And we have discovered ways we can walk away from the shame as we choose our new direction into Christ's love for us.

But what happens after the deliverance? Is it all smooth sailing through the rest of life? It would be nice if it were, but that's almost never the case. We live in the real world where people are volatile and rarely predictable. That's especially true when you experience a powerful, life altering deliverance.

I've heard it said, and I believe it's true that, *"Everything God creates, He tests."* When you read from the first page of the Bible to the last, one of the strongest threads running through the whole of Scripture is that God tests His creation.

God really is a master refiner, looking for the pure and the perfect. Now, none of us can reliably say we're perfect. That's not God's point. He's moving us toward that end, lovingly prodding us toward His kingdom. As we encounter trials in this life, we are always given a choice. Will we run toward the love of Christ and His deliverance, or will we run toward self-interest and operate out of our own strength?

God's after a body of people who are robust, sturdy, and able to endure the trials of life. Those are the people who, when they reign with Christ, will do so out of hearts of love.

Chapter 10

LOYALTY AND BETRAYAL

It's all over the place; every time you turn on the television, there's another "reality TV" show. From *"Survivor"* to *"The Apprentice,"* the people change but the behaviors are always the same. First it's a test of loyalty: can the group work together and remain loyal to each other long enough to accomplish whatever their goal is? After a few weeks of that, they break them up to compete against each other, and the betrayals come up. Everyone's out for his or her own success; that's when the shows have their largest audience. Our nation gets its entertainment from watching public betrayals.

Concepts of loyalty are ingrained in us from our earliest days. We don't think in terms of loyalty when we're little kids, but most of us remember our reaction to crude comments about someone in our family out in a schoolyard. We were particularly sensitive to anything said about Mom or Dad. Most of us still are, even if our parents have passed on. If you had an older brother, you remember how he'd come to your defense if another kid started picking on you.

If you were ever part of a fraternity or sorority in college, you know how the loyalty of your other members came in handy once you were out. Some graduates credit their career success to the relationships they were able to leverage off of, all because of their membership in a "frat house" while in college.

Betrayal and our fear of it were picked up at the same time. Many times the fear we carried inside was not concerned with if *we* would be betrayed, but were we in jeopardy of betraying a friend or family member ourself?

This shows up in a humorous way as we mature and live out our adult lives. Have you ever caught yourself, oh - say, cooking dinner at home in your kitchen, doing it the way you like it done, and say to your spouse, "I'm glad my mom can't see how I'm cooking; she'd have a fit." It's good-natured kidding, and your mom probably doesn't care how you cook, but the trigger inside yourself that prompted the remark is that you'd be betraying your mom because you're not doing things her way, the way she taught you.

As we read today's headlines, we know there are far more serious implications to those who keep their loyalty. Elections are won or lost due to someone's loyalty to a political party or candidate.

In the international arena, loyalty to a cause or a faith can be the glue that keeps global alliances together, sometimes for the good of the world, sometimes not. Any betrayal to those causes can destroy their effectiveness. The United States constitution prescribes the penalty of death for those who commit treason. Treason *is* betrayal.

Betrayal is a spiritual issue. When it happens to us, it can cause problems for us, producing shame and disabling our ability to trust. When we've been subject to a betrayal, it robs us of our ability to remain loyal to those we have relationships with. A betrayal hinders us from developing healthy relationships in the first place.

This is where we have to look at what's gone on in our life as Christ has set us free from the bondages of shame and brought us into His freedom. Look in Matthew as Jesus explains the parable of the sower and the soils to His disciples:

"The farmer (sower) plants the Word. Some people are like the seed that falls on the hardened soil of the road. No sooner do they hear the Word than Satan snatches away what has been planted in them.

And some are like the seed that lands in the gravel. When they first hear the Word, they respond with great enthusiasm. But there is such shallow soil of character that when the emotions wear off and some difficulty arrives, there is nothing to show for it.

The seed cast in the weeds represents the ones who hear the kingdom news but are overwhelmed with worries about all the things they have to do and all the things they want to get. The stress strangles what they heard, and nothing comes of it.

But the seed planted in the good earth represents those who hear the Word, embrace it, and produce a harvest beyond their wildest dreams." Mark 4:13-17 The Message Bible

What Jesus was telling his disciples and the rest of us is, when the truth of the gospel, the reality of Christ in our lives, comes into us, be prepared; be good ground. Satan *will come,* just like he did in the garden to Adam and Eve. Difficulties will arise; hold fast to your faith. These things will test our faith and the reality of our deliverance and healing from shame.

Consider it a sheer gift, friends, when tests and challenges come at you from all sides. You know that under pressure, your faith-life is forced into the open and shows its true colors. So don't try to get out of anything prematurely. Let it do its work so you become mature and well-developed, not deficient in any way.
James 1:2-4 The Message Bible

Now let's go back and resume the story of David, Mephibosheth and Ziba. We've got their examples in Scripture to learn from.

Chapter 11

DAVID, MEPHIBOSHETH AND ZIBA

We need to return to the story of King David and his interactions with Mephibosheth and Ziba. Here's a quick recap from where we left off in chapter four.

David was God's chosen to replace Saul. Samuel went to the house of Jesse to find God's anointed. After looking over all of Jesse's other sons, he asks, *"Are all of the young men here?"* David is brought in from shepherding the sheep and receives God's anointing from Samuel.

Forward to the period after Saul's defeat and death at the hands of the Philistines. David was installed as king over Judah. He was God's anointed king over all of Israel, but was presently reigning over Judah.

One of David's sons, Absalom, betrayed his father by leading a rebellion with the Israelites in an attempt to become king in place of his Father. A battle ensued, and Joab, thinking he was acting out of loyalty to David, murdered Absalom. Joab went into David's house and saw David mourning over the death of his son. At this sight, he reproved David.

And Joab was told, "Behold, the king is weeping and mourning for Absalom." So the victory that day was turned into mourning for all the people. For the people heard it said that day, "The king is grieved for his son." And the people stole back into the city that day, as people who are ashamed steal away when they flee in battle. But the king covered his face, and the king cried out with a loud voice, "O my son Absalom, O Absalom, my son, my son!" Then Joab came into the house to the king and said, "Today you have disgraced all your servants who today have saved your life, the lives of your sons and daughters, the lives of your wives and the lives of your concubines, in that you love your enemies and hate your friends. For you have declared today that you regard neither princes nor servants. For I swear by the Lord, if you do not go out, no one will stay with you this night. And that will be worse for you than all the evil that has befallen you from your youth until now." 2 Samuel 19:1-7 NKJV

From there, Israel began to say, "We need to ask the king to come back." Judah was the last, and David is speaking to Judah:

Then King David sent to Zadok and Abiathar the priests, saying, "Speak to the elder of Judah, saying, 'Why are you the last to bring the king back to his house, since the words of all Israel have come to the king, even to his house? You are my brethren, you are my bone and my flesh. Why then are you the last to bring back the king?' and say to Amasa, 'Are you not my bone and my flesh? God do so to me, and more also, if you are not commander of the Army before me continually in place of Joab.'" So he swayed the hearts of all the men of Judah, just as the heart of one man, so that they sent this word to the king: "Return, you and all your servants!" 2 Samuel 19:11-14 NKJV

They welcomed him back at Gilgal. There were 1,000 men from the tribe of Benjamin coming to greet him. Remember Ziba, the servant of Saul's household; he was coming out also.

Mephibosheth was now in control of all of his grandfather Saul's property. Ziba had been Saul's servant;

he was now Mephibosheth's servant, appointed by David. Ziba didn't like this, and he had a plan.

Chapter 12

DECEPTION AND BETRAYAL

We're coming to the heart of the situation, but we need to see some background about how Ziba had been behaving. Let's go back to chapter 16 of 2 Samuel:

Shortly after David passed the crest of the hill, Mephibosheth's steward Ziba met him with a string of pack animals, saddled and loaded with a hundred loaves of bread, a hundred raisin cakes, a hundred baskets of fresh fruit, and a skin of wine. 2 Samuel 16:1 The Message Bible

A steward doesn't own the property he's using; a steward manages someone else's property. David had told Ziba to manage Mephibosheth's property and to bring the wealth to him. The steward of Mephibosheth was waiting to greet him.

Mephibosheth was eating at King David's table every day, he and his family. Who was living on the property he owned? Ziba, the steward. Whose family and servants had all the advantages of that property? Ziba, his family, and his servants, 35 people in all. He was running a business; there were land and crops, houses and cattle. Where was Ziba living? In the stuff; he was enjoying all of it. He was selling the crops and bringing the money to Mephibosheth, but he got to live in it, because Mephibosheth wasn't. It's important to understand this because of what's about to happen.

And the king said to Ziba, "What's all this?" "The donkeys," said Ziba, "are for the king's household to ride, the bread and fruit are for the servants to eat, and the wine is for drinking, especially for those overcome by fatigue in the wilderness."
2 Samuel 16:2 The Message Bible

Ziba had already decided what he was going to say to David. He had this planned out.

The King said, "And where is your master's grandson?" "He stayed in Jerusalem," said Ziba. "He said, 'This is the day Israel is going to restore my grandfather's kingdom to me.'"
2 Samuel 16:3 The Message Bible

You have to understand the severity of what Ziba had just said. He was saying Mephibosheth wasn't there because he was hoping that King David would lose the battle over Judah, and then he would get his grandfather's kingdom back.

Ziba is setting up David *and* Mephibosheth. It was a power play so Ziba could get his own way. Ziba was jealous and angry over the issue of not getting Saul's property for himself and having to remain a servant. So he acted out of deception and selfish ambition to deceive the king.

"Everything that belonged to Mephibosheth," said the king, "is now yours." Ziba said, "How can I ever thank you? I'll be forever in your debt, my master and king; may you always look on me with such kindness!" 2 Samuel 16:4 The Message Bible

Do you understand that when a deception comes, it has the seeds of betrayal with it? You may not be the target of the betrayal; someone else might be the victim. But in this case, Ziba was betraying *both* David and Mephibosheth.

Chapter 13

THE DEFIANCE OF THE BETRAYER

We'll get to the actions and deceptions of Ziba shortly, but we need to fill in some background information to really catch the dynamics of the situation.

For people who are in the business of writing, no matter whether it's fiction or non-fiction, one of their primary interests is in knowing the "behind-the-scenes" information, or what is usually called the "back-story." It's by knowing this information that they can write about people in the most authentic way. By understanding what came before, they can better communicate what is going on now.

In the Bible, those "back-stories" are usually there. We need to know those stories to understand what's going on behind the scenes. The accounts of what took place before are needed to understand what's going on now. This is where we're beginning.

Let's catch up. King David was running from his own son, Absalom.

Absalom had been born to David from his marriage to Maacah, the daughter of Talmai, king of Geshur. This was during the time that the house of Saul was at war with the house of David. The time of this was right before David began to reign as king of Judah in Hebron, beginning in 1011 B. C.

Because of the deception of a half brother, Amnon, who eventually raped Absalom's sister, Tamar, Absalom burned with bitterness and hatred toward Amnon and had him murdered. This bitterness distorted into a pattern of betrayal against Absalom's own father, David.

Now, Absalom was a good-looking man.

Now in all Israel there was no one who was praised as much as Absalom for his good looks. From the sole of his foot to the crown of his head there was no blemish on him. 2 Samuel 14:25 NKJV

David didn't want to have anything to do with Absalom after the death of David's other son, Amnon. But Absalom wasn't going to have any of that; he wanted to be back in the company of his dad the king. Actually, he wanted to reign as king himself. So Absalom hatched a plan.

As time went on, Absalom took to riding in a horse-drawn chariot, with fifty men running in front of him. Early each morning he would take up his post beside the road at the city gate. When anyone showed up with a case to bring to the king for a decision, Absalom would call him over and say, "Where do you hail from?"

And the answer would come, "Your servant is from one of the tribes of Israel."

Then Absalom would say, "Look, you've got a strong case; but the king isn't going to listen to you." Then he'd say, "Why doesn't someone make me a judge for this country? Anybody with a case could bring it to me and I'd settle things fair and square." Whenever someone would treat him with special honor, he'd shrug it off and treat him like an equal, making him feel important. Absalom did this to everyone who came to do business with the king and stole the hearts of everyone in Israel.
2 Samuel 15:1-6 The Message Bible

Eventually Absalom developed a following and lead a rebellion against David. When David found out that

Absalom had roused the people against him and they were on their way to Jerusalem, David fled into the plains of the wilderness and went up on top of the Mount of Olives to worship and seek God. That's the scene of Ziba's appearance to David where he deceived David into believing that Mephibosheth was ungrateful and hoping for David's defeat so he could claim the throne for himself. That's where we left off with Ziba in the last chapter.

Eventually Absalom and David went out in battle against each other. David commanded one of his captains, Joab, to deal gently with Absalom when they caught him. Joab had other plans and murdered Absalom during the battle.

Of course, David won the battle. God's anointing was on David. No one was going to win against God's chosen.

As David returned to Jerusalem, he came to the Jordan River to cross over. Guess who was there to greet him? You guessed it: Ziba.

At this point, David had already taken back Saul's property from Mephibosheth and transferred it to Ziba. The problem Ziba had was that once one has begun a deception, one has to be diligent to keep it up. Ziba's out there getting a ferryboat to take David and his party back across, trying to do what he thought were good things to do for David.

All of a sudden, guess who else shows up? It's Mephibosheth. Funny how when one is trying to keep a lie going, something just kind of happens to mess it up. That's Ziba's problem now.

Next Mephibosheth, grandson of Saul, arrived from Jerusalem to welcome the king. He hadn't combed his hair or trimmed his beard or washed his clothes from the day the king left until the day he returned safe and sound. The king said, "And why didn't you come with me, Mephibosheth?"

"My master the king," he said, "my servant betrayed me. I told him to saddle my donkey so I could ride it and go with the king, for, as you know, I am lame. And then he lied to you about me. But my master the king has been like one of God's angels: he knew what was right and did it. Wasn't everyone in my father's house doomed? But you took me in and gave me a place at your table. What more could I ever expect or ask?"
2 Samuel 19:26-28 The Message Bible

Now the truth came out. "It was my intention to go with you. I sent my servant to saddle my donkey, and I was going to ride with you. But he betrayed me." The word betrayal specifically means, "to shoot." The betrayer's intent is to kill. Maybe not physically; it could be emotionally, physically, mentally, any way that it can be done. In Ziba's case, he was killing Mephibosheth's reputation in order to steal property for himself.

A betrayal can only happen when you have someone's trust. You can't betray someone who doesn't trust you. If you're my enemy, then I don't have to wonder about whether you want to do good to me. You're going to do everything you can to destroy me. But if you've got my trust, then you have the ability to betray me. Nobody can hurt you like people you love.

The danger is that if you're not careful, you become callous because you're tired of people betraying you. That's very dangerous. None of us can afford to be calloused with people, not while we're living in this world. Some people try to isolate themselves. . . what you've heard called "hermits." They isolate themselves from society; they live out all by themselves, around nobody. They've usually been betrayed over and over; they don't want to go through it again. They isolate themselves and die in all their stuff, or get weird and crazy and become serial killers.

"Betray" means to beguile, deceive, to throw or hurl down, or ultimately to shoot. The word "slander" is interesting. Ziba slandered Mephibosheth. The word "slander," taken from the Hebrew "regal," means to walk along. It's interesting; here's Ziba walking along with his master, who can't walk. It also means "intent, to make a preliminary inspection." In other words, I'm walking along, watching your life, making an inspection of you because I need to find something about you to betray you with. I'm looking for something to use to slander you with.

It doesn't matter what year it is when you're reading this. Do you remember any political conflicts currently, where this very thing has been done?

At my age, I remember the Watergate break-in in the early 1970's. That was done to collect embarrassing information on political rivals so their reputations would be damaged.

Is it within human nature to betray those who are down and now step into favor? Of course it is...to take someone who was down, and looked down upon because no one would even introduce them by name, and then they start getting fame.

The word "fame" means "honor," or "that which brings character." Lots of people who we think are famous aren't really famous; they don't have honor, character, or integrity. You cannot truly carry fame, as God defines fame, unless you're honorable. You might be well known, but you don't have fame in God's eyes because there's no character on the inside. The word is "renown," with honor on your life.

Here was Ziba, representing Mephibosheth, who knew shame, and Ziba couldn't deal with it. Ziba could deal with Mephibosheth when he was a nothing. But now, after his elevation to the king's table, it was not something Ziba could handle.

For we dare not class ourselves or compare ourselves with those who commend themselves. But they, measuring themselves by themselves, and comparing themselves among themselves, are not wise. 2 Corinthians 10:12 NKJV

Ziba was saying, "Now, I've been taking care of Saul's property, but Mephibosheth comes out of nowhere and gets to live in the palace, eat at the king's table, and is given the property I've been tending. It's not fair; he's getting all the honor and I'm not!"

Ziba contrives a plan, which happens when somebody you thought you were better than begins to be honored by God.

David had told Ziba to manage Saul's house and bring the money to Mephibosheth. He agreed, but he didn't like it.

AFTER DELIVERANCE FROM SHAME, HOW THE SEEDS OF BETRAYAL CAN BE PROVOKED IN ANOTHER

Let me give you three things that can get triggered in someone who doesn't have Christ's life through the Holy Spirit residing inside them.

1. When someone is redeemed and restored from shame, it can provoke *envy* in another person.

Envy is discontented desire for someone else's possession or advantages. The synonym is covetousness...to covet what you have. "I want what you have; I don't want what I've got. I've got a nice car of my own, but you've got a nicer one; I want yours. You've got a job that's better than mine, so I want your job; I'm not satisfied with mine anymore." You're an object of envy for them.

The restoration of Mephibosheth from shame to fame provoked envy inside of Ziba. Mephibosheth didn't make Ziba envious. Ziba's heart was inclined to envy when he encountered Mephibosheth's new found fame. All of a sudden the seeds of betrayal started entering his thought processes. Read 2 Corinthians 10:12 from a couple of pages back. Paul wrote that to the Church at Corinth. It can happen to us.

2. When someone is redeemed and restored from shame, it can provoke *jealousy* in another person.

Jealousy is bitter resentment and rivalry. One becomes resentful. A good example might go like this: *"I was blessed when you were saved and delivered from drugs, but now you've got a nice new job, and a new car, and you're married now, and have two kids, and all of a sudden, I'm jealous of you."* Crazy stuff like that. One person's redemption and restoration and prosperity have *nothing* to do with another person's experience in life, other than the testimony of God's grace to us. But as the jealousy begins, the seeds of betrayal get down on the inside.

3. When someone is redeemed and restored from shame, it can provoke *strife* in another person.

Strife means "discord, conflict, struggle, and contention." In Ziba's heart, he was in strife every time he brought the proceeds of the land to Mephibosheth. At this point, Ziba didn't even like Mephibosheth. He wanted to get even; he wanted to get ahead of him. It never entered his mind that he was living better than he had ever dreamed of. He had deserved death; he was at death's door because he had been a servant of Saul. But he was in strife with Mephibosheth. The seeds of betrayal came.

As tragic as betrayal can be, the strength of loyalty is more powerful. We'll look at Mephibosheth's loyalty to David next.

Chapter 14

THE CHALLENGE TO BE LOYAL

Early in this book we looked at events surrounding the relationship between Saul and David. Even when the opportunity for betrayal was present, David's strong loyalty to Saul and his fear of God prevented him from killing Saul.

Loyalty means "the firm allegiance or faithfulness to another." God is faithful to us; He's faithful to watch over His word and perform it. If He said it, will He not do it? He was faithful when you turned your back on Him; He was still faithful to be there to receive you again. God is loyal to His people.

When two or three gather together, God is faithful to be in their midst. He's faithful to us as a people.

The issue is not whether He maintains His faithfulness to us. The issue is, can we be faithful to Him? To be faithful to Christ means that we have *firm allegiance.* It doesn't mean when things are going right, or when good things are happening, or when we're feeling good. It means, we endure whatever comes our way. Our trust in Him, our allegiance, remains strong. Scripture holds great promises for those who endure in the Lord through the trials and temptations of life.

Life is a process of relationships, with God initially, then with our family, outward to our relationships with others in the body of Christ, and continuing out to the rest of the world we come in contact with. Those relationships are held together with trust, which is the opposite of betrayal. Part of the enemy's first deception was to get us to break our trust with God. Satan appealed to pride, and that pulled us away from our trust in God.

In the church I pastor, I received a letter recently from some folks who at one time were active in this church. These were people we had really extended ourselves with. The letter went on, page after page, contending that we hadn't helped enough, and they were leaving. Their attitude was one of, "You just don't care enough!" Now, these were folks we had been up in the middle of the night with. We had spent hour after hour counseling with them. As I read their letter, I realized that the seeds of betrayal were there. My wife and I had been as loyal to them as we knew how, but in their letter to me, they had decided to question my loyalty to them. I thought, "Lord, I have a firm allegiance to these people and their situation, and I'm going to continue to be loyal to them and pray for them and help them." I can't afford under God to do anything but that.

As distressing as this one instance was, it is only one of many similar situations most pastors confront week to week throughout the land. So our question then becomes, "How do you deal with disloyalty?" I have five points.

Next Mephibosheth, grandson of Saul, arrived from Jerusalem to welcome the king. He hadn't combed his hair or trimmed his beard or washed his clothes from the day the king left until the day he returned safe and sound. 2 Samuel 19:24 The Message Bible

Mephibosheth was living in consecration. He refused to live in luxury while the king was at war. His attitude was, "While the king is in jeopardy, I will honor him in my own way." Even though he wanted to be there and was deceived and slandered, he at least could pay the price to seek God on David's behalf.

First, consecrate yourself to loyalty, to the principle of loyalty. Even in the midst of disloyalty, you must consecrate yourself to be loyal. In this very hour, Mephibosheth knew there was disloyalty against his life. In the midst of that, he consecrated himself to be loyal to his king.

"My master the king," he said, "my servant betrayed me. I told him to saddle my donkey so I could ride it and go with the king, for, as you know, I am lame. And then he lied to you about me. But my master the king has been like one of God's angels: he knew what was right and did it. Wasn't everyone in my father's house doomed? But you took me in and gave me a place at your table. What more could I ever expect or ask?"
2 Samuel 19:26-28 The Message Bible

Second, offer the truth; he didn't give anything else. He didn't try to give details. He didn't give a two-hour story. He just said, "I sent my servant to saddle my donkey, but he never came back, and has lied to you."

Just offer the truth. Don't try to declare a doctoral thesis; just tell the truth. "That was not in my heart; that is not what happened. I wanted to be there; my servant went out to saddle it and never came back." Just stop the story. Don't try to defend yourself; just offer the truth.

If someone doesn't believe you, then that's a situation between them and God. If he/she takes you at your word, there's trust, and commitment gets built on that. If he/she doesn't take you at your word, then that person doesn't trust you and is not committed to you.

103

"And he lied to you about me. But my master the king has been like one of God's angels: he knew what was right and did it."
2 Samuel 19:27 The Message Bible

Third, you must declare trust and submission. A lot of people don't understand submission. Our trust and submission are part of our loyalty. If you have trust in someone, your pastor for example, you will have peace when sharing with him, and receive whatever direction or correction with joy.

I have a simple rule for knowing if I am trusting someone or if someone is trusting me: Trust *feels like peace.* If, in the midst of relating to someone, I experience peace, trust is present in that relationship.

If you're declaring your trust to someone (in Mephibosheth's case, it was trusting a king), submission will not be a struggle because you know you're not in the hands of someone who will violate that trust.

Now, submission has become a dangerous buzzword in the body of Christ over the last 30 years. Depending on your background, you may have suffered deep wounds from some unfortunate applications of that word.

Imagine this: "Keep in mind that some who have been given the very power of God have raised armies, defeated the enemy, brought forth mighty works of God, preached and prophesied with unparalleled power and eloquence. . . and thrown spears, and hated people, and attacked others, and plotted to kill, and prophesied naked, and even consulted witches." That's a description of King Saul, from *"A Tale of Three Kings"* by Gene Edwards.

Who would want to be submitted to that? The nation of Israel did, that's who. But glory to God, what came after was the man who God said had a heart after His own: David. When it's a man or woman whose heart has been formed by God, there's someone you can trust *and* submit to.

Sometimes it's the other way around. If you don't like what is being said to you, if you get angry when you're confronted by the Word of God, what's being dealt with in your life is a disobedience you don't want to repent of. Go to the Lord, repent, and turn away from that old attitude and behavior. It's amazing how quickly that mean old pastor you used to not want to hear from can be your best friend.

"Wasn't everyone in my father's house doomed? But you took me in and gave me a place at your table. What more could I ever expect or ask?" 2 Samuel 19:28 The Message Bible

Fourth, even when there's disloyalty, you've got to say, "You don't owe me anything." Mephibosheth was saying to David, "All I had was the right to be killed, because I was from the household of Saul, and his disobedience brought shame on all of us. I'm not going to make any appeals to you. I know what was said about me. But I'm making no appeals. You owe me nothing."

We live in a nation and society today where so many are walking around with a chip on their shoulder. Many feel that everyone owes them something. You have to get to the place where you can say, "Nobody owes me anything."

I don't loan money to people. I used to. But I decided that I would never get caught in that trap again. If I can't give it to you, you can't get it from me. I'm trying to get to the place where nobody owes *me* anything. Mephibosheth told David, "You don't owe me anything."

You've got to get to the place where you don't owe anything. We're not talking specifically about financial issues here, although it's good counsel to become debt free. A debt free lifestyle is an incredible freedom.

> *"That's enough," said the king. "Say no more. Here's my decision: you and Ziba divide the property between you."*
> *Mephibosheth said, "Oh, let him have it all! All I care about is that my master the king is home safe and sound!"*

2 Samuel 19:29-30 The Message Bible

Fifth, demonstrate your gratefulness. Grateful people have problems receiving the seed of betrayal and becoming disloyal.

People who realize all that God has given them and come to a place where no one owes them anything and they don't owe anyone else are thankful for the everyday provision of God. Be grateful. Declare trust and submission. Offer the truth. Consecrate yourself to loyalty.

This last study about David, Ziba and Mephibosheth dealt with who would be loyal, and who was betraying loyalty. We don't have any evidence to know what happened between Ziba and Mephibosheth after that encounter with David.

I believe Mephibosheth continued to live out his life in honor. David's promise to him to always eat at the king's table was never rescinded. He continued to have his place in the king's palace.

My guess is that Ziba died a lonely, discouraged, bitter man when it was all over.

The principle of loyalty is the strength of relationship. That means we're going to make it.

Living Free

We could have used any number of different stories from Scripture. From Adam and Eve, Rahab the harlot, to the woman at the well, the Bible is populated with people who were dealing with shame in their life. Any of these stories could have been the vehicle to guide us through issues of shame and recovery.

Why Mephibosheth and David? Because through them we were able to look beyond the point of restoration from shame, to a typical situation that can develop after a person is redeemed and restored. It's important to understand what can happen next. That understanding can help us guard against the enemy robbing us of our freedom from shame.

It's not enough to know freedom. We must acquire the wisdom to continue in that freedom.

And take the helmet of salvation, and the sword of the Spirit, which is the word of God. Ephesians 6:17 NKJV

Paul's encouragement to the Ephesians was to *wear* the helmet of salvation. It's a helmet because it has to do with covering our heads, our minds, our understanding. From our new understanding, we can now shield ourselves from attacks of the enemy and live free in Christ.

Go forth, seek the Lord and His salvation, and enjoy your freedom.

A Necessary Addition

When I finished the previous page I truly believed that this book was complete. But God has a way a changing our plans and our outcomes. In God's province, that's a good thing.

I've been concerned with the issues of shame and guilt affecting the Body of Christ for several years now. It was that concern that gave birth to this teaching. Only after delivering this teaching before my own congregation in Tulsa, Oklahoma, did I experience an urging from the Lord to address a further condition of shame and guilt in the Church at large.

The decision to leave this as a separate section was deliberate. That's for the benefit of some readers who will be focusing only on this part of the book. Some of the points raised in this section echo earlier chapters.

Had I placed this section into the regular sequence of the book, it would appear after chapter seven. My encouragement is that you would go back to chapters eight and nine after reading this chapter.

I've also included a bit of research to make the point that you, or someone close to you, is in bondage right now.

Chapter 15

A CHURCH IN CRISIS

A criticism of the Church today is that it has lost its moral authority to speak to society at large. It has "lost its voice" in the world. That loss of voice, as well as the bondage brought onto the Church as a result, has left the Church in crisis.

Many of us are suffering from shame due either to a personal bondage we experience or because of those we know and love who are in bondage.

It's the bondage of addictions. For years, the Church has ministered to people who have addictions...drug addiction, alcohol addiction, all manner of substance addictions. These ministry efforts have largely been directed to those outside the Church and to those entering into the church as they recognize their need for repentance and forgiveness from God.

Now the Church, and all of us as part of the Body of Christ, must turn to confront the addiction and the shame that has infected us who are part of the Church.

THE HIDDEN ADDICTION

"We know that perhaps as many as 25% of men in the church are struggling with sexual addiction. We know that one in four women has been sexually abused by the time they're 18 years of age. . .

If those are the people in our pews, and we know they're struggling with sexuality, but we cannot talk openly to them

about sexuality and help them find God's healing, where are they going to go? They either go to the culture and make a bad situation worse, or they remain in silence and Satan has a field day."
Christopher McCluskey, Christian Psychotherapist; co-author of "When Two Become One"

Let me make the point further. As you read the following statistics, keep in mind they refer *specifically* to those in the Church.

First, fifty-one percent (51%) of pastors say cyberporn is a possible temptation. Thirty-seven percent (37%) say it is a current struggle. ("Christianity Today," leadership Survey, December 2001)

Second, nearly eighteen percent (17.8%) of all "born again" Christian adults in America have visited a sexually oriented website. (Zogby survey conducted for Focus on the Family, 2000)

Third, sixty-three percent (63%) of men attending "Men, Romance & Integrity Seminars" admit to struggling with porn in the past year. Two-thirds (66%) are in church leadership and 10% are pastors. ("Pastor's Family Bulletin," Focus on the Family, March 2000)

Fourth, one in seven calls to Focus on the Family's Pastoral Care hotline is about Internet pornography. ("Pastor's Family Bulletin," Focus on the Family, March 2000)

Fifth, forty-seven percent (47%) of Christians admit that pornography is a major problem in their homes. (Internet Filter Review, "Pornography Statistics 2003")

Sixth, one in five born-again Christians believes that viewing magazines with nudity and sexually explicit pictures is morally acceptable. (Barna Research Group, "Morality Continues to Decay," 11/3/2003)

Seventh, thirty-six percent (36%) of Christians say co-habitation is morally acceptable, and thirty-nine percent

(39%) define sexual fantasies as morally acceptable. (Barna Research Group. "Morality Continues to Decay," 11/3/2003)

Some of the losses reported by sexual addicts include:

- loss of partner or spouse 70%
- loss of career 27%
- unwanted pregnancies 40%
- suicidal tendencies 72%
- exposure to AIDS and venereal disease 68%
- legal repercussions 58%

Are you shocked yet? I am. I had no idea of the perverseness of the problem until I ran across these numbers. Maybe you're not shocked. Maybe the statistics include you.

The point here is not to condemn, but to light the path to release you from this shame and bondage. I want to address how this gets started, and point to your freedom in Christ from those dark areas that have you bound up. Follow the very words of Christ after He left the wilderness and the temptations of the enemy:

So He came to Nazareth, where he had been brought up. And as His custom was, He went into the synagogue on the Sabbath day, and stood up to read. And He was handed the book of the prophet Isaiah. And when He had opened the book, He found the place where it was written:

"The Spirit of the Lord is upon Me.
Because He has anointed Me
To preach the gospel to the poor;
He has sent Me to heal the brokenhearted,

To proclaim liberty to the captives
And recovery of sight to the blind,
To set at liberty those who are oppressed,
To proclaim the acceptable year of the Lord."

    Then He closed the book, and gave it back to the attendant and sat down. And the eyes of all who were in the synagogue were fixed on Him. And he began to say to them, "Today this Scripture is fulfilled in your hearing." Luke 4:16-21 NKJV

    Christ's first words to the Church, which for Him at that moment were the Jews, were promises to heal the brokenhearted, proclaim liberty to the captives and recovery of sight to the blind. Two things have never changed: that the Church has those in it who are blind, captive, and brokenhearted, and Christ's promise of healing, liberty, and recovery of sight.

    Quote from Dr. Christopher McCluskey is found on the Elucida Learning website homepage at http://www.elucidalearning.com and is available for viewing online.

    Statistics of losses due to sexual addiction are from the Elucida Learning website. Learning Center, Sexual Addiction, Information you NEED to know at http://www.elucidalearning.com/cartgenie/pg_Learning12-05_Video.asp and is available for viewing online.

    Statistics on Porn and Sex Addiction are from Be Broken Ministries website at http://www.bebroken.com/bbm/resources/articles/stats.shtml and is available for viewing online.

Chapter 16

HOW DID IT BEGIN?

As born-again children of God, we started our life with God by responding to His voice inside our heart. That tug in our heart, what some call the "quickening" of the Holy Spirit in us, was the tangible evidence of our knowledge of God Himself speaking to us. Our initial approach to Christ in repentance was our obedience to His voice in our life. Our life in Christ began as we obeyed His voice and began to trust Him with our life. From that moment of trust, we began to receive the indwelling of His Spirit in our heart.

Back in the Garden of Eden, God told Adam and Eve He would provide everything for them…all their needs, all their desires. It pleased God to have all creation serve them. His only command was to not eat of the tree of knowledge. When they did that, they were listening to the voice of another.

We know the story. When they listened to the lying voice of the enemy, they were choosing to hear, trust, and obey a voice that was not God's. Their own voice, and that of the enemy urging them on, drove them into disobedience.

That's what an addiction is. It's a voice inside us. Pull the word apart: ad-diction, diction-voice. It's a voice that speaks to us that we submit to. We get the word diction, or speech. Addictive behavior is thought to be unmanageable. The reality is when a substance (word or voice) takes over until it dominates your mind and your emotions, you eventually succumb (with your will) to the *idea* that you have no control over your behavior. Thus, the cycle of addictive behavior, which leads to guilt, and then shame, begins.

> *"It happens so regularly that it's predictable. The moment I decide to do good, sin is there to trip me up. I truly delight in God's commands, but it's pretty obvious that not all of me joins in that delight. Parts of me covertly rebel, and just when I least expect it, they take charge.*
> *I've tried everything and nothing helps. I'm at the end of my rope. Is there no one who can do anything for me? Isn't that the real question?"* Romans 7:21-23 The Message Bible

You feel powerless over it. You may feel like it's easier to just turn loose as the lust takes over. Ultimately, this cycle of behavior destroys relationships, marriages, and careers. We are left in a state of shock and defeat.

DEFINING THE ADDICTION

Before launching into what I believe are the controlling influences, let's get clear on what sexual addiction is. By that I mean, what are the characteristics of sexual addiction? Note that these are general characteristics of any addictive behavior.

First, it's a *compulsive* behavior. The sex addict lives with an uncontrolled compulsion to indulge in this behavior.

Second, it's a behavior that the sex addict exhibits *without any regard for consequences.*

Third, it's behavior that the addict is *preoccupied* with. It takes priority over virtually every other area of life.

Fourth, not only is their behavior preoccupying their life, it is *escalating* further dominance over them.

A person may have fallen into sexual sin, have issues that he/she needs to come to Christ and repent of and not technically be an addict. If that's you, keep reading. You aren't off the hook just because you don't fit the classification above. You'll find this material every bit as relevant. Maybe this is the wake-up call you need before your impulses develop into an addiction.

WHY WE ARE INFLUENCED INTO ADDICTION

Go back and reread chapter six. Look at the outside forces that cause us to experience shame. Most of those forces point to one thing: when our heart was wounded.

That wound usually comes when we are very young. The wound is carried in our heart throughout our life. Most everyone, in one way or another, lives life aching from a wound. Several things happened when we received that wound.

One, the wound was an attack on our God-given strength. God has placed strength inside each of us. Since the fall of Adam, one of the many things we've done is to run from that strength.

John Eldredge, in his powerful book, *"Wild at Heart,"* says, "Remember—a man's addictions are the result of his refusing his strength."

This is one of the core dilemmas of a man caught in sexual addiction. He's running to a woman to get strength when he should be going to a woman to *offer* his strength.

Two, the wound was an attack on our identity. Many of us live lives of quiet shame because of an attack on

117

our personal identity. That knowing of who we are deep inside is taken away in shame.

It's difficult for many people to heed the call of Christ on their life, to "lay your life down and follow Him," when they have not yet dealt with issues of personal identity. How can you lay your life down when you aren't sure who *you* are?

Three, the wound left us with a loss of approval. The young boy wants his father to take notice and get excited when he learns to ride a bicycle. A young girl plays dress-up with Mom's shoes and scarves, hoping Dad will notice how beautiful she is. When these events get frustrated or never happen at all, there is a vacuum in the heart.

There's a word that is rarely used but is fitting to describe the impartation of both approval and identity together: approbation.

Approbation is so important in everyone's life that God the Father gave it to Christ at least two times during His life on the earth. First, at the Jordan River when John the Baptist baptized him (Matthew 3:13-17); second, when Jesus was transfigured on the Mount (Matthew 17:1-9).

Do you really believe that Father God wants to withhold that impartation of approval and identity from you?

These three wounds in our heart...the attack on our strength, the attack on our personal identity, and the loss of approval, are the primary things that conspire to push us into addictive behavior, particularly sexual addiction.

THE DECEPTION OF THE ADDICTION

The striving of those trapped in the shame of sexual addiction is an attempt to accomplish a couple of basic things for themselves.

First, any counselor will tell you that what an addict (of any type) is attempting to do is control their environment. Find a good drunk, and you've found someone who thinks he's king of the world. With sex addicts, their behavior provides a feeling of power. It's a contradiction; the behavior leaves them feeling powerless, but the behavior acted out is an attempt to feel in control.

Second, any area of life outside of faith and trust in Christ Jesus is an arena of life without peace. As a contrast, when we are caught up in times of worship to God, we experience wonderful moments of refreshing peace. However, when we live in those other areas of our life where we are not trusting God, we have no peace. We make frantic efforts to control life. We wind up striving to achieve peace in our life out of our own strength. It always fails. This is where most addictive behavior begins.

Chapter 17

IT ALL COMES BACK TO CHRIST

The end of addictive behavior happens when we finally address the wounds inside. Most were received at a very young age, and most were an attack on our identity.

Now when the tempter came to Him, he said, "If You are the son of God. . ." Matthew 4:3 NKJV

Then the devil took Him up into the holy city, set Him on the pinnacle of the temple and said to Him, "If You are the Son of God. . ." Matthew 4:5-6 NKJV

And again the devil took Him up on an exceedingly high mountain and showed him all the kingdoms of the world and their glory. And he said to Him, "All these things I will give You if You will fall down and worship me." Matthew 4:8-9 NKJV

The enemy's assault on Christ in the wilderness was primarily an attack on His identity. Twice Satan challenged Christ's identity, and the last temptation was an attempt to have Christ surrender His strength. All were attempts to get Christ to compromise His trust in His Father.

THE ISSUE OF TRUST

If we've not trusted God in an area of our life, what have we done? We've become suspicious of Him, that's what. We've refused to trust Him because we have suspicions about His heart toward us. The old nature in us is always suspicious. That was the premise the enemy had for tempting Adam and Eve in the Garden of Eden.

KNOWING CHRIST

Nothing is more important than trusting Christ with your life. Why have we as Christians not turned to Him completely? Why don't we know Him with every part of our being, turning all of our life over to Him?

It has to do with whether or not we really want to know and trust Christ.

They came to the edge of the village where they were headed. He acted as if He were going on, but they pressed Him: "Stay and have supper with us. It's nearly evening; the day is done." So He went in with them. And here is what happened: He sat down at the table with them. Taking the bread, He blessed and broke and gave it to them. At that moment, open-eyed, wide-eyed, they recognized Him. And then He disappeared.

Back and forth they talked. "Didn't we feel on fire as He conversed with us on the road, as He opened up the Scriptures for us?" Luke 24:28-32 The Message Bible

If we are to know Christ, we must not only receive His blessing, but we must also be willing to receive His breaking, for with the breaking we are given a revelation of Him. It is only then that we recognize Him as Lord.

Out of our imagination and our soul's fear, that suspicion we've carried inside ourselves, we distance ourselves from Him, thinking He would reject us on close inspection of our life. That's part of the original deception of the enemy.

How little we know that to be broken by Christ is to know Him, experience Him as our life.

THE REALITY OF BROKENNESS

Some of you have almost decided to stop reading here. I hope you're still with me. This is your chance to see what brokenness really is.

The last chapter began identifying God's voice in our life, and the voice of addiction in our life. The choice of whose voice we listen to and obey centers around who we will trust, and who we will be suspicious of.

To be broken before God is simply to choose to respond with trust when we've heard His voice confronting us with our self. That "pricking of the heart," when we know God is challenging us to turn to Him, is, again, His voice inside us and our certain awareness of that. Christ's call is to come into freedom and have our eyes opened by His Spirit.

Go back to the last page of chapter 15. Reread Luke 4:16-21. This is Christ's fulfillment of the prophet Isaiah, that He has come to give sight to the blind, set the captives free, and heal the brokenhearted. Now go back and reread chapters eight and nine. Know that as we begin to trust the voice of Christ inside and turn away from the voices of the enemy and our old self, He will release us to know Him. Only as we know Him will we receive our identity as sons and daughters of the King.

We end as we began:

IF CHRIST SAYS YOU'RE A KING, YOU ARE!

ABOUT THE AUTHOR

Gary McIntosh is the Founding Pastor and President of Greenwood Christian Center, Inc. and Greenwood Enterprises, Inc. Greenwood Christian Center is now Transformation Church, a dynamic, multi-ethnic, multi-cultural, non-denominational ministry in Tulsa, Oklahoma. TC embraces the spirit of its founder as it expresses a radical, diversified, progressive, 21st century technological church. Pastor McIntosh has functioned in full-time ministry for the past forty two (42) years as a pastor, an overseer, preacher, teacher, and educator throughout this nation.

Gary W. McIntosh is a graduate of Oral Roberts University, where he was identified as a part of the "Who's Who Among College Students." Upon graduation, he served in several administrative and Chaplain positions within the University as Director of the Chaplain's Office and Associate Chaplain of Oral Roberts University, associate pastor of Bethany, in Baton Rouge, Louisiana, and co pastor of Higher Dimensions in Tulsa, Oklahoma.

Gary W. McIntosh has conducted numerous seminars regarding leadership development and has taught the principles of church pioneering. He has provided pastoral oversight for numerous ministries across the nation, and has assisted pastors in establishment of administrative excellence within their ministries. The workshops and seminars that he has taught have been comprehensive in training pastors on the dynamics of church growth, conflict resolution, staff development, marriage enrichment and economic empowerment, and church consulting, just to name a few areas of his vast expertise.

Bishop McIntosh resides in Tulsa, Oklahoma, with his wife of forty years, Debbie, and four children: Angela, Joshua, Samuel and Alanda, and three grandchildren: Juliane, Malorie, and Madison.

Gary W. McIntosh has authored several books, to include:

Ministers in Training Manual,
Strategic Operations Seminar,
Arrows of Victory,
Disappointment to Destiny,
Where the River Flows,
And his new book: From Shame to Fame

This current book along with all of
the above titles are available directly from:

Transformation Church
1519 W. Pine St.
Tulsa, OK 74127-3510
(918) 582-3580
or online at: mcintoshministries.org

Made in the USA
San Bernardino, CA
07 January 2017